IMAGES
of America

SCHAFER STATE PARK

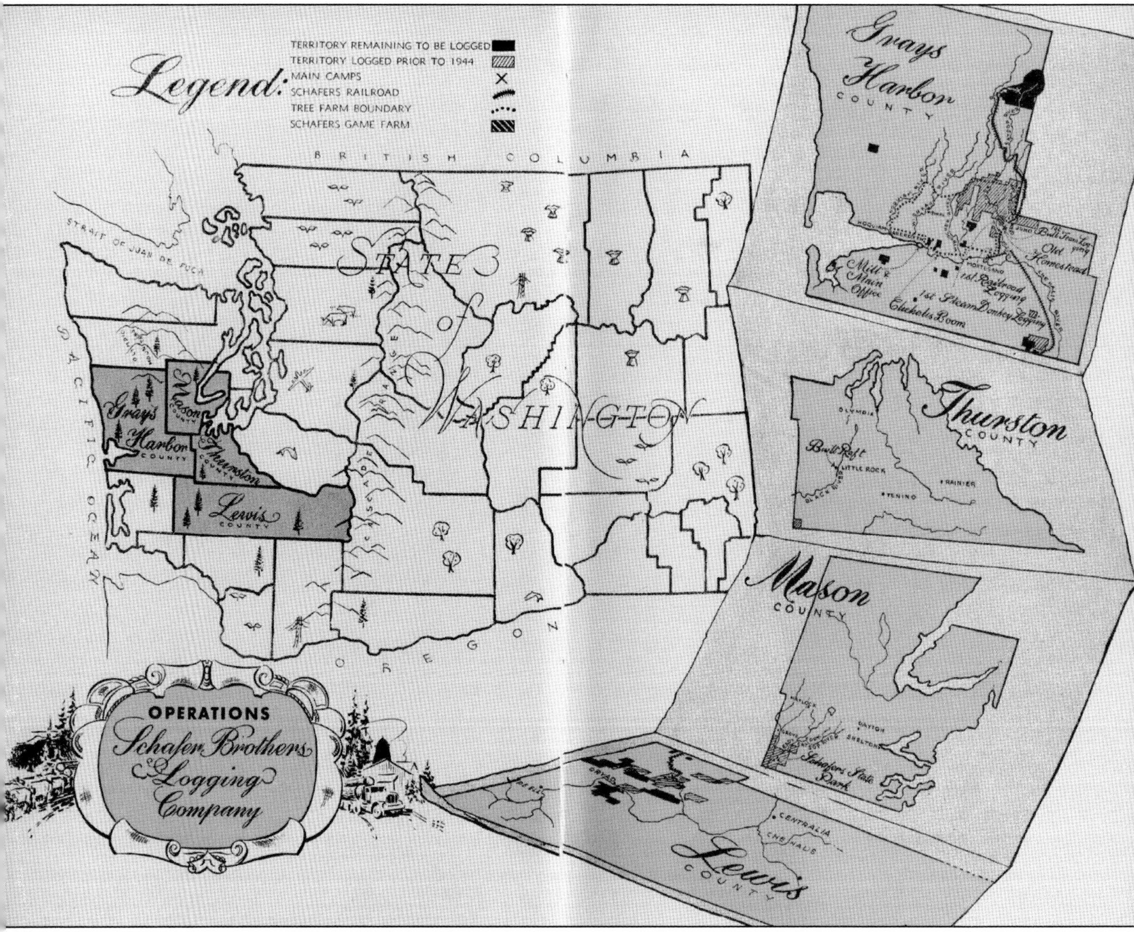

By the end of World War II, the Schafer Bros. Company logging operation covered four counties in southwestern Washington State. This graphic appeared in 1945 in the book *Narrative of Schafer Bros. Logging Company's Half Century in the Timber* by well-known Pacific Northwest historian Stewart Holbrook, which is now long out of print. (*Half Century in the Timber.*)

On the Cover: A Schafer Bros. Company employee picnic in the 1920s would not have been complete without a bathing beauty contest. These ladies stand on one of the structures built for the event at Schafer State Park on August 14, 1927, and they are ready for judging. The winner received recognition as well as a choice item donated by a local store. (Chehalis Museum.)

IMAGES
of America

SCHAFER STATE PARK

Peter Schafer Reid
and Barbara Seal Ogle

ARCADIA
PUBLISHING

ISBN 978-0-7385-9642-6

Published by Arcadia Publishing
Charleston, South Carolina

Printed in the United States of America

Library of Congress Control Number: 2012945088

For all general information, please contact Arcadia Publishing:
Telephone 843-853-2070
Fax 843-853-0044
E-mail sales@arcadiapublishing.com
For customer service and orders:
Toll-Free 1-888-313-2665

Visit us on the Internet at www.arcadiapublishing.com

In the hope that the next generation will enjoy local history as much as we have, we dedicate this book to Ada, Hadleigh, Brian, and Paul.

Contents

ACKNOWLEDGMENTS

Many people helped make this book possible, however, the authors are responsible for any errors or omissions. Our thanks to Betty and Cliff Perry; Stetson Palmer; Trina Young; Sue Schafer; Jerry Handfield and Mary Hammer, Washington State Archives; Pat Smith; Anne Scroggs; Pat Clemons; University of Washington Libraries Special Collections; Chehalis Valley History Museum; Janet Anderson; Tom and Kathleen Schafer; Dann Sears, Aberdeen Museum of History; John Reid; Terri Middleton; Pete Replinger; Rose Mary Moore; Garold Messenger; Alex McMurry; Mark Vetter; and our editor, Amy Kline at Arcadia Publishing

For convenience, the following abbreviations will be used for image attribution: University of Washington Libraries Photograph Collection 516, Clark Kinsey (UW Libraries, C. Kinsey No.); Jones Photograph Collection of Anderson Middleton Company (Jones No.); Anita and Bud Fuquay Collection (Fuquay); Washington State Archives (State Archives); Betty Perry Collection (Perry); Schafer Family Collection (Schafer); Aberdeen Museum of History (Aberdeen Museum); Chehalis Valley History Museum (Chehalis Museum); and the Sue Schafer Collection (Sue Schafer).

INTRODUCTION

In 1871, John D. and Anna Schafer arrived in Olympia, Washington, from the Midwest by way of San Francisco and Victoria, British Columbia. They came with their children, including their son Peter, as well as members of the Muller family, from Anna's first marriage, and John's son, Dionis (Dennis), from his first marriage. The rest of the group included members of the Anton Kramer, William Koch, and Charles Schrader families.

Shortly after their arrival, John Schafer and others built a raft, filled it with provisions, and set forth down the Black River to find a place to homestead. After several mishaps, including swamping the raft and being rescued by local Native Americans, they managed to get the provisions to a spot six miles upriver from the mouth of the Satsop River. There, John built a crude shelter and returned to Olympia to retrieve his family. After a two-day ride in a horse-drawn wagon, the family arrived at the homestead. They immediately set to work and soon had the property cleared and a reasonable cabin built. By 1879, two more brothers were born, Hubert and Albert, who would go on to join Peter to form the Schafer Bros. Company.

Soon, the Schafer homestead on the Satsop became a center for settlers, hunters, and timber cruisers coming into the area. Two local Native Americans made a pair of large dugout canoes that were always available to ferry visitors across the river. Anna Schafer provided good basic food for the many visitors coming and going. The family worked the land for the next 14 years until 1893, when the three boys convinced their parents to let them try logging. Within a few years, with crews of friends, Muller family relatives, and local Native Americans Billy Quiack, Amos Comenout, and Hyasman, logging of the Satsop area was underway. The life of these early pioneer settlers of the Satsop River Valley has been documented in Sue Schafer's recently published *Voices from the Past: John Dennis Schafer Family Letters, 1842–1898*, made up of John D. Schafer's letters to his relatives in Germany.

The Native American census in the late 1800s found only a small number of the Satsop Tribe still alive in the area. As a consequence, natives of the area were required to select other tribes for affiliation. The Satsop residents had a choice of the Quinault or the Lower Chehalis tribes. Most chose the Quinault, and many of their descendants are members of the Quinault Nation today. Despite the small population, there was a tribal reservation on the southwest side of the park from the late 1800s until the mid-1900s. A tribal cemetery remains today on the former reservation land.

Within a few years, the Schafer logging operation had moved on from bull-team logging to new methods: machine logging with a steam donkey engine and cables. By 1910, they had three large steam donkeys working. The next big escalation in their logging practices came in 1913, when they stopped floating logs down the Satsop River and set up a railroad operation to bring their logs out of the woods. The next year, the brothers incorporated as the Schafer Bros. Company, with a capitalization of $300,000.

At the peak of their operation, the Schafers were running one of the largest logging, milling, and shipping concerns in the Pacific Northwest. A glance at their properties and equipment at this time, not including ships and tugs, shows five sawmills in operation, which were served by numerous camps sending logs over 100 miles of rail. The rail system required 18 locomotives, 70 donkey engines, 325 logging cars, and approximately 3,000 employees. From 1893 to 1924, the Schafer Bros. Company logging operation traversed the whole history of logging methods in use during that time before expanding into sawmills, door manufacturing plants, railroads, and cargo ships.

During World War I, the US military found it difficult to obtain enough specialty wood products to meet the needs for aircraft building. In response, Col. Bryce Disque established the Army Spruce Division to recruit and enlist loggers into the Army. The Schafer Bros. Company was reportedly the first logging company to procure soldiers to work in the woods in 1917. Of the 100 men employed, the majority worked at Schafer Camp Five, near what became Schafer State Park.

In 1909, the State of Washington built a fish hatchery adjacent to the future Schafer State Park after a hatchery built at the confluence of the Satsop and Chehalis Rivers in 1898 had failed. The state discovered that the area about six miles upriver on the Satsop was much more fruitful and built the new hatchery there. That part of the river was so productive that the hatchery broke every Washington State record by producing 21,591,000 fish eggs in 1916. The area continued to be productive, and two more hatcheries were built a few miles upriver. From 1950 to 1960, the Washington State Department of Fisheries maintained the fish weir below the bridge at the park and harvested fish eggs for the hatchery at Bingham Creek.

This area of the Satsop River had long been known as a prime fishing spot for the Native American tribes of the Chehalis Valley. The Schafers had had a close relationship with the local Native Americans since John D. Schafer was rescued by them when his raft tipped over. Canoes were provided to the family and Native Americans were part of the early logging crews set up by the Schafer brothers. It is likely that tribal members let the Schafers know of the excellent fishing around the area.

The 1920s saw considerable expansion of the Schafer Bros. Company operations. The land for the park was donated and opportunities for entertaining customers were developed, with the company establishing a game farm near the park for hunting and purchasing a yacht to provide tours. Each of the three brothers built new homes; Peter and Hubert's in Aberdeen and Albert's in Montesano. They also built summer homes on Hood Canal in Mason County—not far from the park—where Anna Schafer had loved to go berry picking in the early 1900s.

In 1922, the brothers decided to pay tribute to their parents, John D. Schafer, who had died in 1898, and Anna Schafer, who had died in 1909, by donating the land for Schafer State Park. At a ceremony on the spot, the Schafer Bros. Company presented to the City of Montesano 25 acres of wonderful old-growth virgin fir forest for use as a public park. The Montesano Chamber of Commerce had facilitated the gift and helped celebrate the opening in 1922. No deed was executed at this time, but over the next two years, it was decided that it would be better to donate the land to the state park system rather than to the city. The area had particular meaning to the brothers because the family had often fished and picnicked there in the early years, and it is located about three miles upriver from the original Schafer homestead. In the early 1900s, volunteers built a dance hall, which the Montesano Chamber of Commerce built a roof for in 1923.

On February 23, 1924, the Schafers executed a deed to the State of Washington for the land to be used as a state park. The park contained 500-year-old trees that offered an image of what the Schafer family had seen in the area when they arrived in 1871. It was the first donation of land for a park by anyone connected with the timber industry, and it joined with previous donations by private individuals and groups to help build the state park system, which began in 1913.

Over the years, the park became a popular spot for picnics and was used by many large groups from the area. The Schafer Bros. Company hosted annual employee picnics there that were attended by up to 6,000 people. Not only were there many logging and lumbering contests, such as high climbing, log rolling, log bucking, shingle packing, and log inspecting, but also races and contests, such as boys' and girls' swimming races, a canoe race, a tug-of-war contest, and pie-eating contests. In addition, there were special employee contests for the man with the shiniest dome and the oldest female employee as well as a race for single ladies and a race for married ladies, with prizes offered by local merchants. The Schafer Bros. Company also sponsored its own band to provide entertainment at the annual picnics. Other groups who held large picnics at the park included the Farm Bureau, with over 3,000 attendees; the Montesano Business Men; the Scandinavian Central Committee; the Order of Reineberg; the Germania Club; and Vasa Lodge.

In the early 1930s, work continued on renovating existing amenities and building new ones. Workmen were recruited from the County Charity Commission and funding was obtained from the Civil Works Administration (CWA). Early in 1933, with funds from the State Parks Commission and under the supervision of Fred Russell, this crew built three brick camp stoves, five eight-foot tables, two 60-foot tables, three 48-foot tables, and two small kitchens, and repaired the restrooms. At the end of the CWA program, it was reformed from simply a job-providing entity into the Washington Emergency Relief Administration (WERA), the local agency of the Federal Emergency Relief Administration (FERA).

In the mid-1930s, the Works Progress Administration (WPA) was brought in to construct buildings in the park. The WPA assumed the work of FERA, which was terminated in 1935, and was designed to offer work to the unemployed on an unprecedented scale by spending money on a wide variety of programs, including highways and building construction, slum clearance, reforestation, and rural rehabilitation. Between 1933 and 1938, at least $16,731 was obtained from the WPA and the FERA to improve Schafer State Park. With these funds, it was possible to build the ranger's residence, two comfort stations, a registration booth, two kitchens, a drinking fountain, and a water system.

In 1936, the *Montesano Vidette* reported, "All buildings constructed on this project are of material gathered in the Park: rocks from the Satsop River and timbers, roofing, windows and doors from native fir and cedar." The use of washed river rock in Depression-era facilities is unique, particularly since the National Park Service advised against it due to the supposed instability of the materials. However, at Schafer State Park, the use of these materials lends a notable cohesion to the built features of the park. For example, the sloping windowsills of larger river cobbles, very uniform in size, are consistent throughout the park buildings.

Meanwhile, even though the number of mills in Aberdeen had declined from 37 to nine, the Schafer Bros. Company continued extensive logging and lumber operations during the Depression years. The employee picnics continued at the park and other Schafer family events were held there, at the logging camps, and at Hood Canal.

In the 1940s, little work was undertaken at the park, as World War II and its aftermath required the attention of the entire population. Despite the war, the Schafer Bros. Company continued to maintain good relations with employees by holding annual banquets, supporting the employee picnics, and paying fair wages. In 1945, at the end of the war, the sons of Peter, Hubert, and Albert Schafer purchased the famous Alderbrook Inn on Hood Canal, making many improvements on it over the next decade. In recent years, the resort has been taken over by executives of the Microsoft Corporation and substantially rebuilt.

In the early 1950s, the leadership of the Schafer Bros. Company came to the conclusion that they were unable to continue operating the company and needed to sell. In 1955, the Schafer Bros. Company completed the sale of all its holdings to the Simpson Timber Company of Shelton, Washington. Shortly after the sale, Carl Schafer, a son of Peter Schafer, took over Schafer Game Farm and turned it into a museum. The museum was made up largely of items he had retained from Schafer logging operations, such as photographs, tools, trucks, and even a railroad engine. Carl operated the museum until his death. Today, most of the items from the museum are found at the Chehalis Valley History Museum in Montesano.

The 1950s saw a new burst of energy and interest in improvements for Schafer State Park. Superintendent C.C. "Doc" Palmer rebuilt the kitchens on the day-use and camp sides of the park and built the entrance monuments between 1950 and 1953. By this time, the dance hall had become unusable and was taken down. In 1953, it was replaced with a pavilion that was open on three sides with an enormous river rock fireplace set into the end wall.

In 1946 and 1951, additional land was added to the park through purchases from the Creamer and Nuxoll families, totaling 42.74 acres. On January 8, 1953, the Schafer family executed a deed transferring 53 acres of additional land for the park, but it was not finalized until January 1955, when a formal presentation was made. With this last gift, the park's size was increased to its present 119.57 acres.

In the 1970s, Schafer State Park became the site for annual reunions of people who had worked in the Civilian Conservation Corps (CCC) in western Washington. The events continued into the 1980s, by which time so few remained alive that the reunions were discontinued. In the late 1990s, Chapter 64 of the National Association of Civilian Conservation Corps Alumni, based in Tacoma, erected a monument at Schafer State Park dedicated to Pres. Franklin D. Roosevelt for his effort in establishing the CCC. In the 1930s, the 982nd Company Camp of the CCC operated in nearby Elma.

In recent years, because of state financial difficulties, Schafer State Park has been under the threat of closure or transfer to another entity. Reduction in funding has also led to the use of many volunteers to help maintain the park. Nearby residents have stepped forward and provided much-needed labor and equipment to keep the park in peak condition. In 2009, a group of friends of the park joined with friends of nearby Lake Sylvia State Park to form Friends of Schafer and Lake Sylvia State Parks (FOSLS). With oversight from FOSLS, the future of Schafer State Park looks good indeed. In 2010, FOSLS gained added support in securing the future of Schafer State Park when it was identified as a place of statewide interest and entered in the State and National Registers of Historic Places.

One

Pioneer Days in the Satsop River Valley

Members of the original Schafer family are seen here with the original homestead in the background, across the Satsop River. Standing, from left to right, are Mrs. Comfort; her daughter, Mrs. Carl Wicks; Dennis Schafer; Hubert Schafer, with wildcat in hand; Peter Schafer; and John D. Schafer. In the wagon, from left to right, are Herman Muller; Albert Schafer; Anna Schafer, the wife of John D.; and Mr. and Mrs. Chris Muller on the seat. (Jones No. 24,662.)

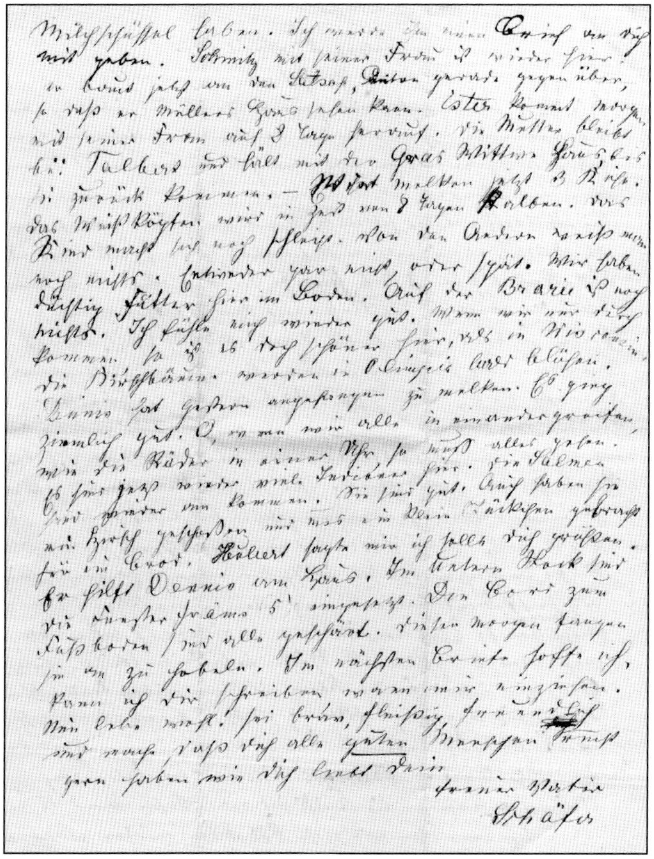

This letter by John D. Schafer to his daughter Gretchen was written in German in 1873. It is translated into English below. The Schafer family had arrived at their homestead on the Satsop River only a few months before, but John was already struck by the beauty of the area and the possibility of a fruitful life on the river. He writes that he thinks it may be more beautiful than their home area in Wisconsin. (Both, Sue Schafer.)

We have very much food in the ground here. On the prairie there is nothing yet. I am feeling well again. If we can persevere then it is more beautiful here than in Wisconsin. Soon, the cherry trees will bloom in Olympia. Dennis started to milk yesterday. It went quite well. Oh, if we all work together, like the wheels in a watch, then everything goes well. There are many Indians here again. The salmon is about to return. It is good. They shot a deer and gave us a small piece for bread. Hubert told me to give you his regards. He is helping Dennis with the house. On the lower floor the window frames (five) are set in place. The boards for the floor are all uneven. This morning they will start to plane them. In the next letter I hope to be able to tell you when we will move in. Good-bye now!

Be good, diligent, friendly and behave such that all *good* people will like you just as does your faithful father Schäfer

The Schafer family intended to obtain ownership of the property they claimed under the Homestead Act, which required the land to be worked and improved for several years. Once the time limit had passed and the required improvements made, title would be granted to the homesteaders. This document represents the initial claim signed by John D. Schafer 14 months after his arrival on the Satsop River. (Sue Schafer.)

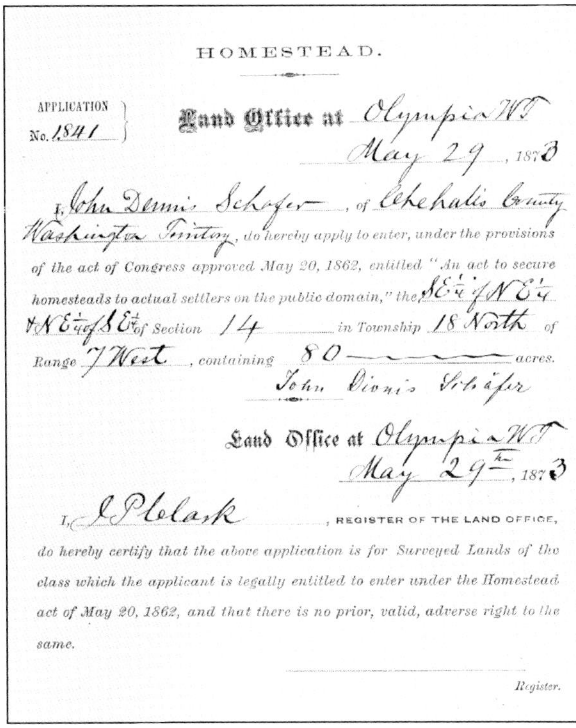

HOMESTEAD.

APPLICATION No. 1841

Land Office at Olympia W.T. May 29, 1873

I, John Dennis Schafer, of Chehalis County Washington Territory, do hereby apply to enter, under the provisions of the act of Congress approved May 20, 1862, entitled "An act to secure homesteads to actual settlers on the public domain," the SE¼ of NE¼ & NE¼ of SE¼ of Section 14 in Township 18 North of Range 7 West, containing 80 acres.

John Dionis Schäfer

Land Office at Olympia W.T. May 29th, 1873

I, J. P. Clark, REGISTER OF THE LAND OFFICE, do hereby certify that the above application is for Surveyed Lands of the class which the applicant is legally entitled to enter under the Homestead act of May 20, 1862, and that there is no prior, valid, adverse right to the same.

Register.

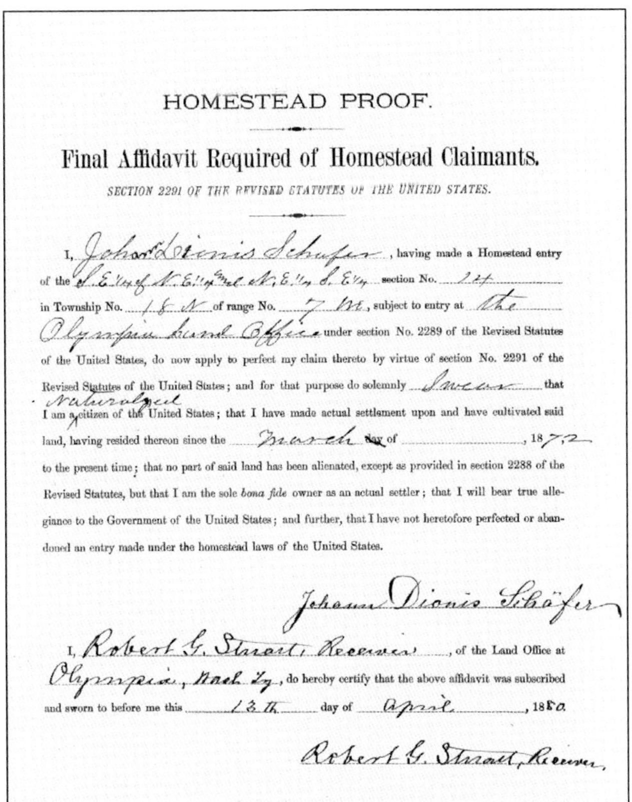

HOMESTEAD PROOF.

Final Affidavit Required of Homestead Claimants.

SECTION 2291 OF THE REVISED STATUTES OF THE UNITED STATES.

I, John Dionis Schafer, having made a Homestead entry of the S.E.¼ of N.E.¼ and N.E.¼ S.E.¼ section No. 14 in Township No. 18 N of range No. 7 W, subject to entry at the Olympia Land Office under section No. 2289 of the Revised Statutes of the United States, do now apply to perfect my claim thereto by virtue of section No. 2291 of the Revised Statutes of the United States; and for that purpose do solemnly swear that I am a naturalized citizen of the United States; that I have made actual settlement upon and have cultivated said land, having resided thereon since the March day of, 1872 to the present time; that no part of said land has been alienated, except as provided in section 2288 of the Revised Statutes, but that I am the sole *bona fide* owner as an actual settler; that I will bear true allegiance to the Government of the United States; and further, that I have not heretofore perfected or abandoned an entry made under the homestead laws of the United States.

Johann Dionis Schäfer

I, Robert G. Stuart, Receiver, of the Land Office at Olympia, Wash. Ty., do hereby certify that the above affidavit was subscribed and sworn to before me this 13th day of April, 1880.

Robert G. Stuart, Receiver.

John D. Schafer was able to perfect his title to the land seven years after filing his claim under the Homestead Act. He had been born in Germany and needed to become a naturalized citizen in order to make the claim. In addition to the claim papers, he was required to file a copy of his naturalization certificate. This proof of claim shows that the family settled on the land in 1872 and lived on it and cultivated it thereafter. (Sue Schafer.)

Anna Bollenbeck Muller married John D. Schafer on October 4, 1868. She had been married previously to Reiner Muller, who died, and had three children—Chris, Christine, and Julie Muller—who accompanied the Schafer family to settle along the Satsop River. Anna grew up on the Bollenbeck farm in Wisconsin and lived from 1841 to 1909. (Sue Schafer.)

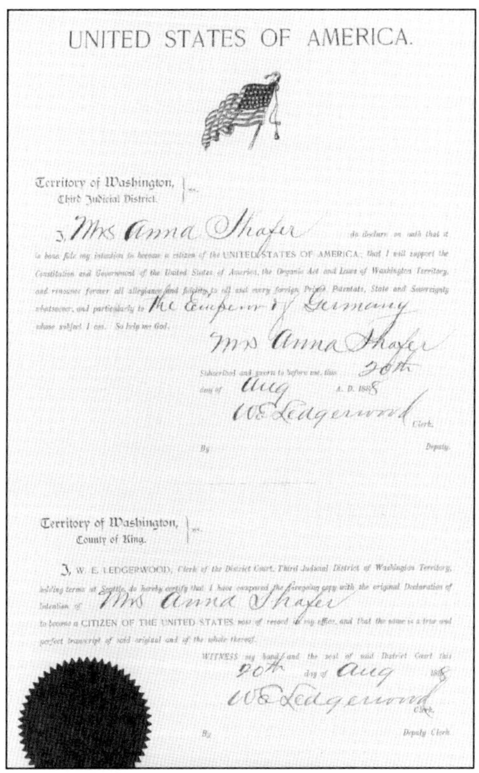

UNITED STATES OF AMERICA.

Territory of Washington, } ss.
Third Judicial District.

I, Mrs Anna Shafer do declare on oath that it is bona fide my intention to become a citizen of the UNITED STATES OF AMERICA; that I will support the Constitution and Government of the United States of America, the Organic Act and Laws of Washington Territory, and renounce forever all allegiance and fidelity to all and every foreign Prince, Potentate, State and Sovereignty whatsoever, and particularly to the Emperor of Germany whose subject I am. So help me God.

Mrs Anna Shafer

Subscribed and sworn to before me, this 20th day of Aug A. D. 1888

W E Ledgerwood, Clerk.

By Deputy.

Territory of Washington, } ss.
County of King.

I, W. E. LEDGERWOOD, Clerk of the District Court, Third Judicial District of Washington Territory, holding terms at Seattle, do hereby certify that I have compared the foregoing copy with the original Declaration of Intention of Mrs Anna Shafer to become a CITIZEN OF THE UNITED STATES now of record in my office, and that the same is a true and perfect transcript of said original and of the whole thereof.

WITNESS my hand and the seal of said District Court this 20th day of Aug 1888

W E Ledgerwood, Clerk.

By Deputy Clerk.

Although Anna Schafer had lived in Wisconsin for many years before coming to the Satsop River Valley, she did not submit her application to become a citizen of the United States until 1888, in the Washington Territory. (Sue Schafer.)

This 1890s photograph shows the Schafer family home, which was built in 1895. From left to right are Louis, Peter, and Chris Muller; their parents, Chris and Amelia Muller, holding their baby daughter Anna; John D. and Anna Schafer; John and Anna Schafer; their parents, Marie and Peter Schafer, holding their baby son, Carl; and Herman Muller on the extreme right. A pet elk is tied to the front fence. (Fuquay.)

The Temperlys were another early pioneer family in the Satsop River Valley. They are seen here in front of the log cabin they built. Log cabins were somewhat unusual in the valley after families had lived on the land for a few years. Once the need for an initial building was satisfied, the pioneers tended to build the kind of farmhouses they had known in the Midwest. (Perry.)

Relations between the pioneer families and members of local Native American families were quite good. In this studio photograph, two of the Schafer family members pose with two local Native Americans. Standing from left to right are Billy Quiack, Hubert Schafer, and Amos Comenout. Herman Muller is seated. (Sue Schafer.)

This studio photograph of Peter Schafer is from the 1890s. While he lived in a pioneer setting with few amenities and spent most of his time in the woods cutting down the huge fir trees in the area, he still managed to obtain a formal suit, a hat, and impressive accessories for this photograph. (Sue Schafer.)

Despite living a grueling pioneer life, formal family portraits were important events for the Schafer family. In this photograph from the 1890s, the three boys, Albert, Hubert, and Peter, stand behind their parents, Anna and John D. Schafer. At this point, John D., who died in 1898, had only a short time to live. (Jones No. 11,322.)

Although many of the early photographs contained formal poses, sometimes the photographer and the subjects decided on more colorful scenes. Here, from left to right, are Peter Schafer, before he grew a mustache; Dio Reinig, a cousin; and Hubert Schafer. (Sue Schafer.)

Still in their teens, Albert Schafer and his cousin Herman Muller are seen here in highly sophisticated formal suits with vests and, for Albert, an impressive keychain. The photograph was likely taken in a studio in Montesano. (Sue Schafer.)

Dennis Schafer was the son of John D. Schafer by his first wife, Elizabeth. Dennis married Laura Mouncier in the late 1880s. The couple is seen here with their children, Addie, Gretchen, Ida, and Ernest, in 1896. Ernest died shortly after the photograph was taken. Dennis and Laura's descendants, the Vetter family, still farm along the Satsop River near Schafer State Park. (Mark Vetter.)

Early pioneer family members picnic in the Satsop River Valley in 1900. Several members of the Gleason, Muller, and Schafer families are seen, including Peter Schafer, sitting second from the right. (Perry.)

The Gleason farm remained under the management of one family for more than 150 years, longer than any other farm in the valley. At one time, the farm contained more than 450 acres. This photograph of the barn was taken around 1900. (Perry.)

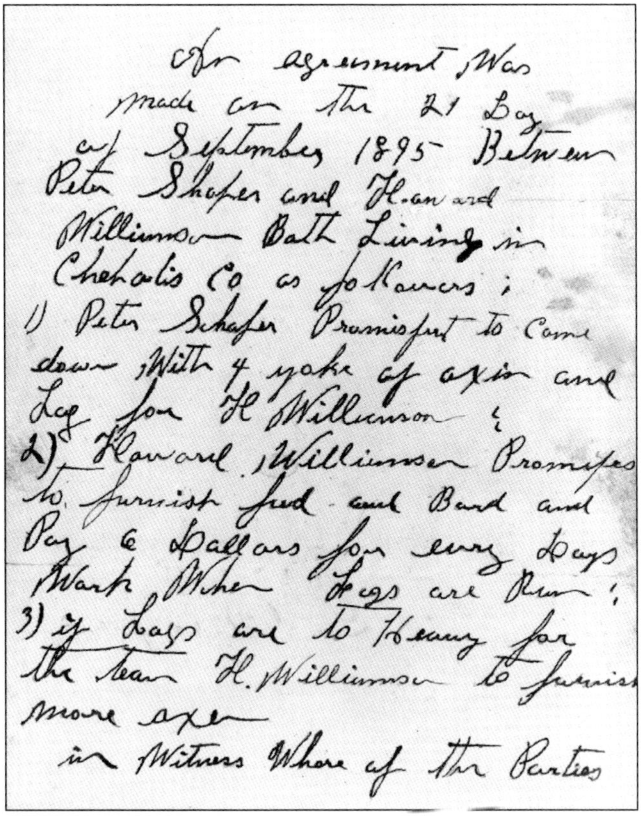

An agreement Was
made on the 21 Day
of September 1895 Between
Peter Shafer and Howard
Williamson Both Living in
Chehalis Co as follows;
1) Peter Schafer Promisfut to Come
down With 4 yoke of oxin and
Log for H Williamson;
2) Howard Williamson Promises
to furnish feed and Bord and
Pay 6 Dallars for every Days
Work When Logs are Run;
3) if Logs are to Heavy for
the team H. Williamson to furnish
more oxen
in Witness Whereof the Parties

The Schafer brothers' logging operations began between 1893 and 1895, with the oldest son, Peter, leading the way. This contract, dated September 21, 1895, is one of the earliest records of their operation. In it, Peter agrees to bring four yoke of oxen and log Howard Williamson's property. (Fuquay.)

The enormous size of the logs being taken in 1898 can be seen in the logjam below in the Satsop River. Seen here are, from left to right, ? Hyasman, Hubert Schafer, Albert Schafer, Ed Kesterson, Herman Muller, Peter Schafer, Ben Kesterson, and John Minkler. Even a dog got into the act. (Fuquay.)

By 1897, Peter Schafer and his brothers were well on the way to their logging careers. Here, Peter, the bull puncher, stands on the right with his goad stick in hand. Roy Gill, riding on one of the bulls, was the skid greaser. The team of five pairs of oxen would be expected to haul the great trees to the river, where they could be floated to market. (Jones No. 14,647.)

By the late 1890s, the Schafers had earned enough money logging to hire 20 men and build a primitive camp for them. In the camp building, there were no springs or mattresses; instead, hay or fir boughs were used for the beds, an open fire in the middle of the room provided heat, and a hole in the roof carried the smoke outside. Hubert Schafer sits in front on the left, and Native American Billy Quiack sits in the second row on the far left. (Chehalis Museum.)

By 1900, the Schafers were able to purchase a small steam donkey to haul the logs out of the woods. The donkey engine had been invented in California in the early 1800s. With its long cables, it could move logs great distances. Seen here, from left to right, are August Maas, Peter Schafer, and Hubert Schafer. (Fuquay.)

The Satsop River is not a large river, and for much of the year there was insufficient water to carry the huge logs to market. At these times, the logs would be hauled to the river, where they might remain for several months, waiting for the river to rise. Here, members of the Schafer crew stand on logs on the shore with a lady visitor (far right). (Chehalis Museum.)

Seen here are two of the local Native Americans who worked for the Schafers in the early days. Amos Comenout is standing on the left and Billy Quiack is in the middle, standing on the springboard. Hubert Schafer is sitting on the far right, and two lady visitors are on each side of the tree. (Sue Schafer.)

This log has been swiped—the end cut—and hewed along the "ride" side to make it easier to pull along the skid road. It is now ready for the oxen to be hooked on to pull it to the river. From left to right, John Minkler, Hubert Schafer, and Ben Kesterson are seen at work about 1898. (Sue Schafer.)

Family Tree, Descendants of Jim Klu-was'la-kut and Lucy Chinaskit

Jim Klu-was'la-kut b.1835 in what is now Grays Harbor County d.n/a		Albert Comenout b.1892-d.n/a
married under Native American custom prior to 1857 ⇒	Amos Comenout b.1857-d.1915	Johannah Comenout b. 1893-d.n/a
Lucy Chinaskit b.n/a-d.1871	m.n/a ⇒	Addie Comenout b. 1897-d.n/a
	Annie Charley b.1877-d.n/a	Isabella Comenout b. 1899-d.1960
		Allen Comenout b.about 1899-d.before 1926
		Charles Comenout b.1900-d.1960
		William Comenout b.1903-d.1972
		Maud Comenout b.1903-d.n/a
		Edward Amos Comenout Sr. b.1905-d.1929
		Elsie Comenout b.1906-d.n/a

In the late 1800s, Native American ladies joined in the desire for professional studio photographs. In the photograph below are, from left to right, (first row) Belle Comenout and Edna Comenout; (second row) Florence Strom and Hannah Comenout. The Comenout children joined the Schafer children and the children of other pioneer families at the Schafer School, along the Satsop River. (Both, Rose Mary Moore, a descendant of Jim Klu-was'la-kut and Lucy Chinaskit.)

Two

Life and Logging Before and During World War I

Shortly after Hubert Schafer returned from a trip to Germany, Bertha Thornton of Aberdeen agreed to marry him. This wedding photograph, taken before 1910, includes, among others, the married couple; Hubert's mother, Anna, in the dark dress on the right; and his brother Peter, third from the right in the back row. (Sue Schafer.)

This Schafer logging crew poses with a donkey engine on the Satsop River in the early 1900s. The two ladies were likely not part of the crew but perhaps visitors for the day. Native Americans Billy Quiack and Amos Comenout are on the far left and far right, respectively. (Chehalis Museum.)

Logjams were a perennial problem for the Schafer loggers on the Satsop River. The oxen could tow the logs from the forest to the river, but if the river was low, the logs would be dumped in the river to wait for high water after the rains came, and then moved downriver. The best logging season was in the dry months, which was unfortunately when the river was at its lowest. (Fuquay.)

In the late 1800s, the Schafers established a school near their home on the Satsop River. Children from the surrounding area attended the school, and it was considered part of the state school system. In these photographs, classes pose near the well-built schoolhouse. Teacher Helen Gleason (below, far right) was a descendant of early pioneer Daniel Gleason. (Above, Chehalis Museum; below, Perry.)

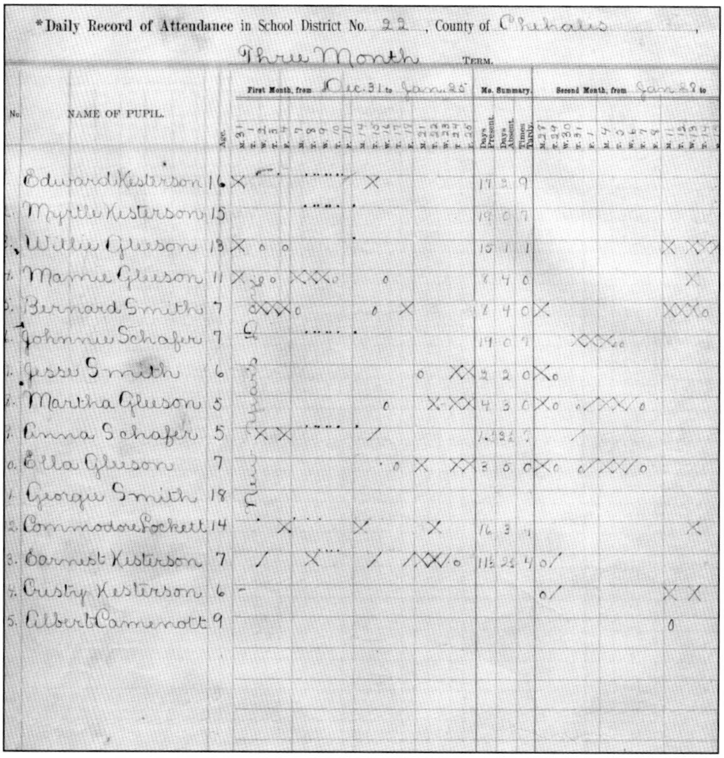

*Daily Record of Attendance in School District No. 22, County of Chehalis

Three Month Term.

No.	Name of Pupil	Age
	Edward Kesterson	16
	Myrtle Kesterson	15
	Willie Gleason	13
	Mamie Gleason	11
	Bernard Smith	7
	Johnnie Schafer	7
	Jessie Smith	6
	Martha Gleason	5
	Anna Schafer	5
	Ella Gleason	7
	George Smith	18
	Commodore Lockett	14
	Earnest Kesterson	7
	Custy Kesterson	6
	Albert Camenott	9

This attendance record from the Schafer School in 1900 demonstrates the comprehensiveness of the school's records. Eldridge Wheeler was the first teacher at the school, which was originally a small log building. Wheeler would board with neighbors for a week or two while he was teaching. He was also one of the main speakers at the dedication of Schafer State Park. (Perry.)

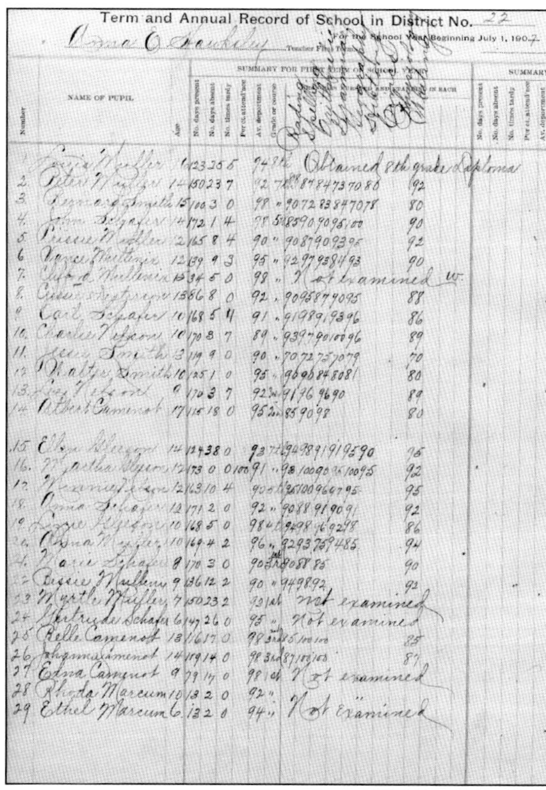

Term and Annual Record of School in District No. 22

For the School Year Beginning July 1, 1907.

In 1900, Peter Schafer's children, John "Jonnie" and Anna, were in the school along with several Gleason children, the descendants of pioneer James Gleason and his nephews; several Kesterson children, the descendants of early logger Ben Kesterson; and Amos Comenout, part of the large Native American family living in the area. This 1907 grade report shows a much larger class, with students' ages ranging from six to 16 years old. The names of Peter Schafer's younger children, Carl, Marie, and Gertrude, appear along with several Comenout and Muller children. The names of a number of new families in the area also appear. Especially interesting are the grades received by the students in the various subjects. (Perry.)

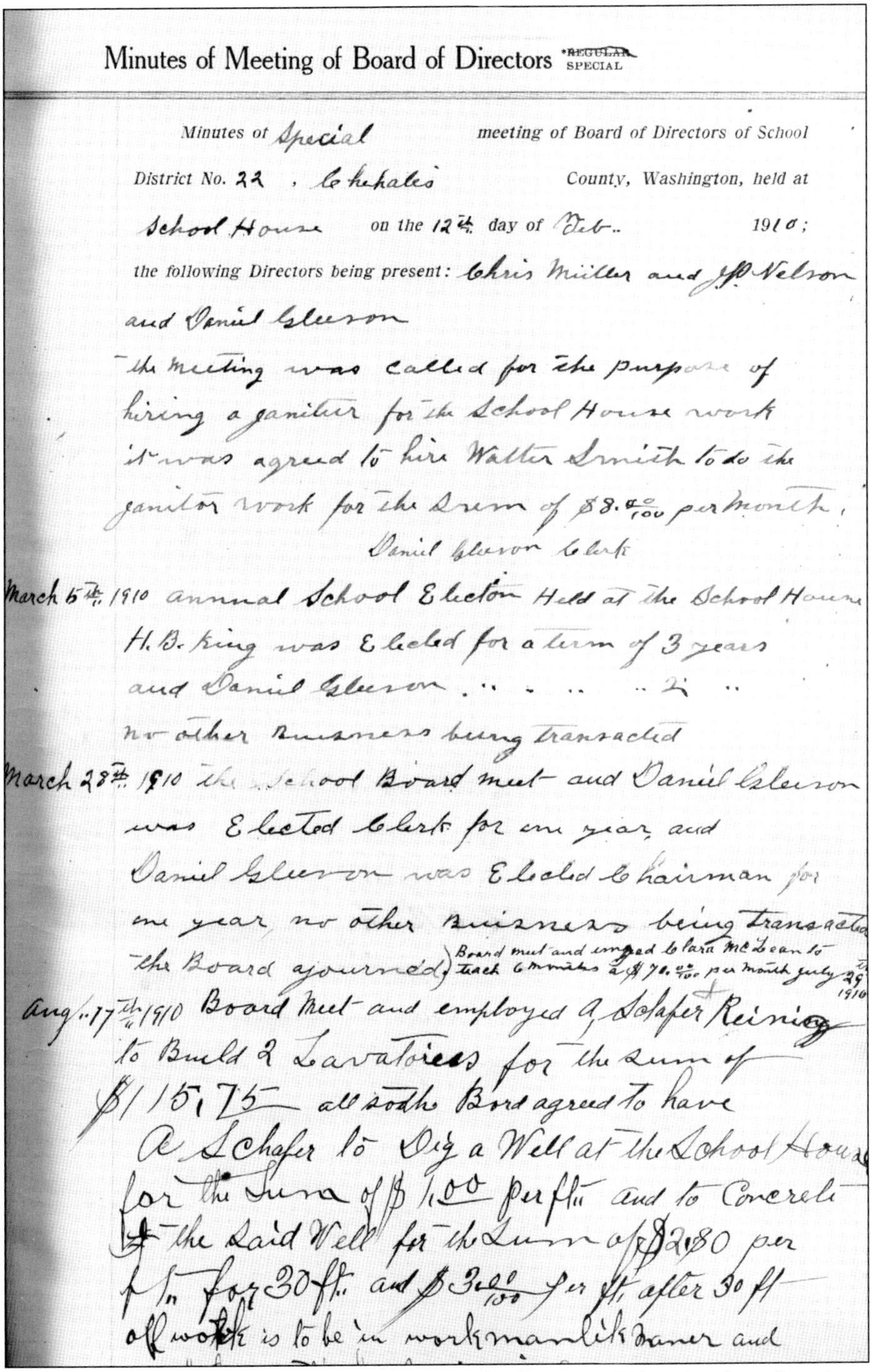

Minutes of Meeting of Board of Directors ~~REGULAR~~ SPECIAL

Minutes of Special meeting of Board of Directors of School District No. 22, Chehalis County, Washington, held at School House on the 12th day of Feb. 1910; the following Directors being present: Chris Miller and J.P. Nelson and Daniel Gleeson

the meeting was called for the purpose of hiring a janitor for the School House work it was agreed to hire Walter Smith to do the janitor work for the sum of $8.00/100 per month.

Daniel Gleeson Clerk

March 5th 1910 annual School Election Held at the School House H. B. King was Elected for a term of 3 years and Daniel Gleeson " " " " 2 "

no other business being transacted

March 28th 1910 the School Board met and Daniel Gleeson was Elected Clerk for one year and Daniel Gleeson was Elected Chairman for one year no other business being transacted the Board ajourned) Board met and employed Clara McLean to teach 6 months at $70.00/100 per month July 29th 1910

Aug. 17th 1910 Board Meet and employed A. Schafer Reinig to Build 2 Lavatories for the sum of $115.75 all so the Bord agreed to have A Schafer to Dig a Well at the School House for the Sum of $1.00 per ft. and to Concrete the Said Well for the Sum of $2.80 per ft. for 30 ft. and $3.00/100 per ft. after 30 ft. all work is to be in workmanlike maner and

The minutes of the Schafer School board meetings for the year 1910 make clear that the school was a part of the public system, in District 22 for Chehalis County. Grays Harbor County was later carved out of Chehalis County. While the minutes cover four meetings for the year, they are remarkable for their brevity. The costs for salaries and equipment are also illuminating—the janitor's salary was $8 per month and two lavatories were built for $115. (Perry.)

In October 1905, it was time to bring in crops at the Schafer farm. Relatives, friends, and neighbors were gathered together for the threshing. Anna Schafer is in the foreground wearing a white apron. Although there are no oxen, two handsome white horses have been brought in to help with the threshing. (Aberdeen Museum.)

This 1906 photograph shows Anna Hawksly's parents at their home near Matlock, a few miles north of the early Schafer homestead. Anna Hawksly married Pat Griffin, who was a pioneer from County Limerick, Ireland, and was the brother of Laura Griffin Gleason, who had married a descendant of early pioneer James Gleason. Anna went on to become one of the teachers at the Schafer School. (Perry.)

In 1907, several members of the Schafer family traveled to Germany to visit relatives. This photograph of Hubert Schafer on his knee holding the hand of a German lady was converted to a postcard and sent to Bertha Thornton, the woman in Aberdeen he had asked to marry him. The card carried this message: "You had better make up your mind or I will bring this lady back with me." When Hubert returned, Bertha agreed to marry him. A photograph of their marriage party is on page 27. (Sue Schafer.)

John D. Schafer was born in Witterschlick, near Bonn, in the central western part of Germany. In 1907, Peter Schafer and his wife, Marie, traveled to that area to visit relatives. They are seen on the left below with two of their relatives in Witterschlick. (Sue Schafer.)

By the early 1900s, Peter and Marie Schafer's family was complete, with seven children. The family was living in their own house along the Satsop River. Seen here at their home are four of the children; from left to right, they are (first row) Edward and Arnold; (second row) Gertrude and Marie. Arnold was born in 1903 and died young in 1916. (Schafer.)

Studio photographs sometimes went to extreme lengths to seem realistic. In this photograph in an automobile, Bertha Schafer is at the wheel. Her husband, Hubert, is next to her, and in the backseat, Albert Schafer sits between Helen and Justine Carothers. (Sue Schafer.)

By 1910, Peter and Marie Schafer had a comfortable home on the Satsop River where they lived with their seven children. From left to right, they are (first row) Marie, Peter, Arnold, and their daughter Marie; (second row) Edward, John, Gertrude, Anna, and Carl. (Chehalis Museum.)

Young Schafer family members and friends from the Satsop River Valley are seen here in the early 1900s. From left to right, they are (seated) Hubert Schafer, Margaret Detrich, and Albert Schafer; (standing) Lizzie Schmitt and Nellie Kesterson. (Sue Schafer.)

There was a weir for the fish hatchery on the Satsop River at Schafer State Park. The workers could use the weir to trap the fish so the eggs could be removed for hatchery use. In 1914, the hatchery set a state record, producing 21,591,000 fish eggs. Enormous numbers of fish came back to spawn, and a good number surround the workmen in this photograph. These hatchery photographs were taken around 1909. (UW No. 33336, Freshwater and Marine Image Bank.)

This is a photograph of the main fish hatchery building on the Satsop River, next to what would become Schafer State Park. The hatchery contained several buildings, holding ponds, and a weir on the river. This building was torn down in the early 1960s. (Schafer.)

The stylish quintet of teenage girls above poses for a photograph in Montesano in 1911. Daughters of the pioneer Gleason family stand with several of their friends. On the window of the building behind the girls is the name of W.H. Abel, a prominent Grays Harbor attorney. (Perry.)

Helen Gleason, the daughter of Daniel and Johanna Gleason, was known as an intrepid traveler with a thirst for adventure. She is seen here in Alaska in 1914, sitting on the fuselage of one of the bush planes used to traverse the Alaskan wilderness. According to family lore, she may have convinced the pilot to let her fly the plane. (Perry.)

This photograph was taken in the early 1900s in front of the old Gleason farmhouse on the Satsop River, which still stands today. Several members of the Gleason family and their friends are in the car. Johanna Gleason is standing in the doorway. (Perry.)

The Montesano High School class of 1916 poses on the steps of the school. Rose Gleason is in the first row on the far left, and Elizabeth "Beth" Gleason, the daughter of Daniel and Johanna Gleason and mother of Betty Perry, is in the first row on the far right. Carl Schafer is in the fourth row on the far left. (Perry.)

In the years immediately before World War I, trips to the nearby ocean beaches became possible, and it quickly developed into an important destination for the teenage girls of the Satsop River Valley. Marie (second from left) and Gertrude Schafer (fourth from left) and several of the young Gleason girls are seen here at the beach in 1916. (Perry.)

Also in 1916, Gertrude (far left) and Marie (third from left) Schafer, the daughters of Peter and Marie Schafer, pose at the beach with girls from the Gleason family. (Perry.)

This 1916 photograph was taken at the ocean beach west of Aberdeen. The girls were able to stay in one of the cabins there. In this group, Marie Schafer is on the far left and Helen Gleason is on the far right. (Perry.)

The automobile became an important part of life for residents of the Satsop River Valley. Here, in 1919, Helen Gleason sits behind the wheel of a very imposing Packard automobile in front of the Gleason farmhouse. (Perry.)

Hood Canal, in Mason County, was a popular place for visits and picnics. Despite the unpaved roads, one could drive there in about an hour. Seen here around the time of World War I, the women are, from left to right, (first row) Elizabeth "Beth" Gleason, Marie Schafer, Gertrude Schafer, Anna Schafer, and the Schafer girls' mother, Marie Schafer. The gentlemen are unidentified. (Perry.)

Not only did World War I bring young men into the Army and into training, but boys also felt the need to develop their military skills. Here, from left to right, Edward Schafer, Howard Nelson, Harold Nelson, and Ben Muller are fully outfitted and are being put through their paces to demonstrate the necessary military discipline. The two men on the right are unidentified. (Perry.)

During World War I, the US military found it difficult to obtain a sufficient supply of specialty wood products to meet their needs for aircraft building. In response, Col. Bryce Disque established the Army Spruce Division to recruit and enlist loggers into the Army. The Schafer Bros. Company was reportedly the first logging company to procure soldiers to work in the woods in 1917. Of the 100 men employed, the majority worked at Schafer Camp Five, near what became Schafer State Park. An additional feature of the Spruce Division was the founding of the Loyal Legion of Loggers and Lumbermen, known as the 4Ls. It was an employee-owner union that eventually included almost all the lumber owners in the Pacific Northwest and more than 100,000 woodworkers. The 4Ls outlasted the Spruce Division but eventually died out in the 1930s. (Both, State Archives.)

During World War I, many of the men from the Satsop River Valley and the surrounding areas joined the Army. Local man Lloyd Foss, who later married Elizabeth "Beth" Gleason, became an ambulance driver and is seen here with a fellow driver and some of the cars and equipment they used at Camp Dodge, Iowa. (Perry.)

This scene at the Schafer Bros. Camp Four in 1919 demonstrates several unique logging methods. The high lead system used a spar tree that carried cables through blocks high off the ground, a significant improvement over the earlier method of dragging logs along the ground. In crotch-line loading, two tongs are hung from a spreader bar that is controlled by wire cables. (Chehalis Museum.)

In 1919, the Schafer Bros. Company continued to build railroads into the woods to haul out cut logs. The Bucyrus steam shovel played an important role in building the railroad grades. Standing on the bank are, from left to right, Jim Malone, John Schafer, and Walter Robertson. Around this time, usual salaries were $3 per day for men who operated the choker, $4 per day for engineers, and $5 per day for head sawyers. The men usually worked 60-hour weeks. (Chehalis Museum.)

Asahel Curtis was a well-known Pacific Northwest photographer in the first half of the 1900s. This photograph was taken at the famous Paradise Inn in Mount Rainier National Park. It was made into a postcard and mailed to Martha Gleason in Satsop in 1918. (Perry.)

Three

The 1920s Boom and the Establishment of Schafer State Park

The interior of the Peter Schafer home on Hood Canal was a bit unusual, in that it had a large public room with a handsome fireplace at one end, but few separate bedrooms. Instead, the gallery on the second floor contained sleeping porches that could accommodate many young people, separated by gender of course. (Janet Anderson.)

For a number of years into the 1920s, the Schafer Bros. Company operated a general store in Montesano, near its administrative offices. Shortly after this photograph was taken, the store was closed so the Schafers could concentrate on the lumber business. However, they did sell lumber for retail as well as wholesale and also advertised their products in local newspapers. (UW Libraries, C. Kinsey No. 3816.)

In May 1922, Elizabeth "Beth" Gleason married Lloyd Foss, who was from another Satsop River Valley pioneer family. The wedding party is seen here outside the Gleason home along the Satsop River. Beth is second from the left in the front row, and Lloyd is on her left. (Perry.)

Raising one's own food was, of course, a significant part of early life in the Satsop River Valley. Most fowl, including chickens, ducks, turkeys, and geese, were raised as domestic animals. Above, Johanna Gleason feeds the flock in front of the Gleason farmhouse. (Perry.)

The Gleason and Schafer families were two of the earliest families to settle in the Satsop River Valley, and despite many friendships and connections between the families, a formal joining of the families did not occur until the early 1920s, when Timothy Gleason married Anna Schafer. The couple is seen here with their two daughters, Patricia and Gertrude. (Patricia Gleason Smith.)

In the 1920s, the Schafer Bros. Company expanded in many directions. One such development was the purchase of a motor yacht, the *Dreamerie*. These two photographs demonstrate the use of the ship to take customers on hunting expeditions. In the 1920s and 1930s, it was possible to take the ship to remote parts of Washington State and Canada to hunt deer, elk, bear, and other animals. Many customers from Asia and the eastern United States would rarely, if ever, have had such an opportunity until they boarded the *Dreamerie*. (Both, Schafer.)

The Schafers would also take family and friends on cruises around the waters of the Puget Sound, to British Columbia, and even to Alaska. Timothy Gleason (first row, far left) is seen here with unidentified friends and family members on a trip in 1928. (Patricia Gleason Smith.)

Hunting was an important part of life for residents of the valley, and the forests were rife with game and birds. In another effort to boost sales, the Schafer Bros. Company established a game farm near Schafer State Park, where customers could be brought to shoot game. Pheasants and other birds and a herd of elk were maintained on the property for this purpose. From left to right, John Schafer, Edwin Hobi, Peter Schafer, and Edward Schafer are seen with a day's take of birds. (Schafer.)

The ladies were not to be left out of the Schafer family hunting expeditions. Here, Marie Schafer, the daughter of Peter and Marie Schafer, is prepared to join an expedition in full hunting gear with her shotgun and her hunting dog. (Schafer.)

Marie Schafer would leave nothing to chance in her hunt for wild game. She is seen here with her rifle instructor in the 1920s, making sure that in the next hunt she could keep up with her brothers. (Schafer.)

Schafer's Game Farm.

Herd of elk at Schafer's Game Farm.

These two photographs from Stewart Holbrook's *Half Century in the Timber* show the Schafer Game Farm as it looked in the early 1930s, shortly after it was set up. The game farm was a short distance from Schafer State Park and eventually became a small housing development. (*Half Century in the Timber.*)

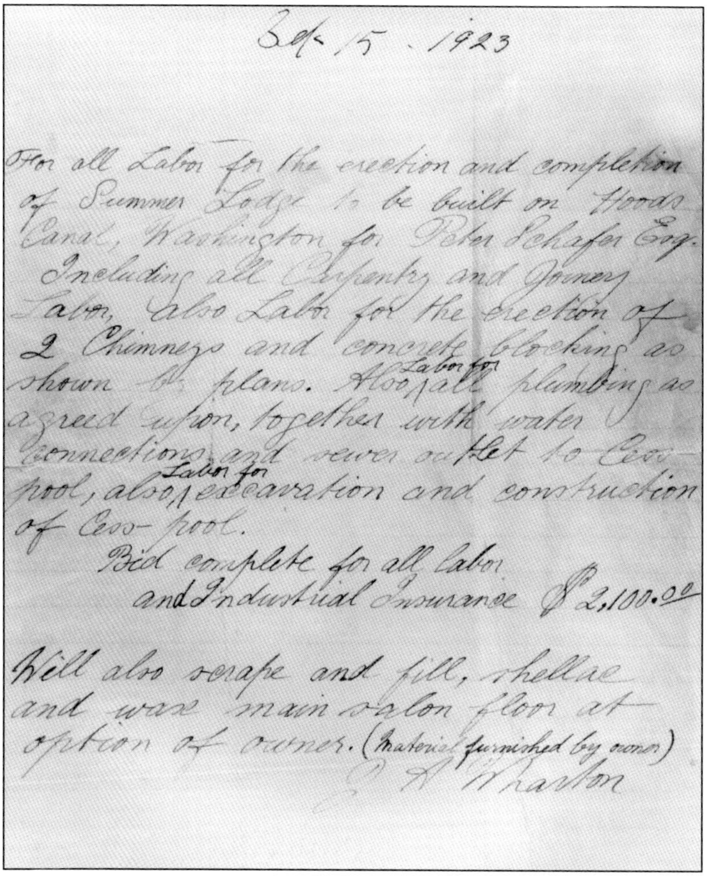

Sep. 15 . 1923

For all Labor for the erection and completion of Summer Lodge to be built on Hoods Canal, Washington for Peter Schafer Esq. Including all Carpentry and Joinery Labor, also Labor for the erection of 2 Chimneys and concrete blocking as shown on plans. Also Labor for all plumbing as agreed upon, together with water connections and sewer outlet to Cess-pool, also Labor for excavation and construction of Cess-pool.

Bid complete for all labor and Industrial Insurance $2,100.00

Will also scrape and fill, shellac and wax main salon floor at option of owner. (material furnished by owner)

[illegible] Wharton

In 1923, Peter Schafer built a large home on Hood Canal, not far from the Schafer homes in the Satsop River Valley. Peter's brothers, Hubert and Albert, also built homes on Hood Canal in the 1920s. Peter's home was divided into two units in the 1940s and given to his two daughters, Anna and Marie. The house (below) still stands today and is owned by the daughters of Anna and Marie. The contract (left) is somewhat remarkable for its brevity and for the modest cost of the house. Since Peter Schafer could provide all the lumber from the company mills, the price was low. (Both, Janet Anderson.)

Edward Schafer, the son of Peter and Marie Schafer, is seen here with a college friend from the University of Washington, ready for a dip in Hood Canal. Peter Schafer's recently built home on Hood Canal is in the background. Some of the sleeping porches can be seen on the second floor. (Schafer.)

Albert Schafer built his home on Hood Canal (below) a few miles down the shore from Peter Schafer's home. While Albert was having lunch with well-known Seattle architect Elizabeth Ayers, they began talking about a summer home. When he returned from the restroom, Ayers showed him a drawing she had made on a matchbook cover of the proposed house, to which Albert reportedly replied, "Let's do it." In the early 1960s, the house appeared on the cover of a brochure for the Chevrolet Corvette. The house is still standing today and is often referred to as the "Castle." (UW Libraries, C. Kinsey No. 3770.)

The 1920s also saw the Schafer brothers and their families moving out of the Satsop River Valley and building homes in larger communities nearby. This house was built in Montesano by Albert and Helen Schafer. It still stands today, although some years ago it was moved a short distance to make room for Grays Harbor County administration buildings. (UW Libraries, C. Kinsey No. 3764.)

Hubert Schafer built his family house in Aberdeen, the major port and largest city in Grays Harbor County. The house stands on a hill overlooking the town and the former Schafer Bros. Company mills. It still stands today. (UW Libraries, C. Kinsey No. 3645.)

By the 1920s, the Schafer Bros. Company had established many logging camps in the Satsop River Valley and the surrounding forests. Some of the camps were small towns with shops, schools, family cabins, and large bunkhouses for the loggers. Other camps were designed as temporary placements and were built on supports so they could be loaded on trucks or railroad cars and moved to the next logging site. The map below, by Pete Replinger, shows several of the camps. Several more camps were established in other nearby areas. The original direction sign above indicates the guidance needed to find the camps in the deep woods as well as the increasing number of camps. Eventually, there were more than 50 camps. (Above, Schafer; below, Pete Replinger.)

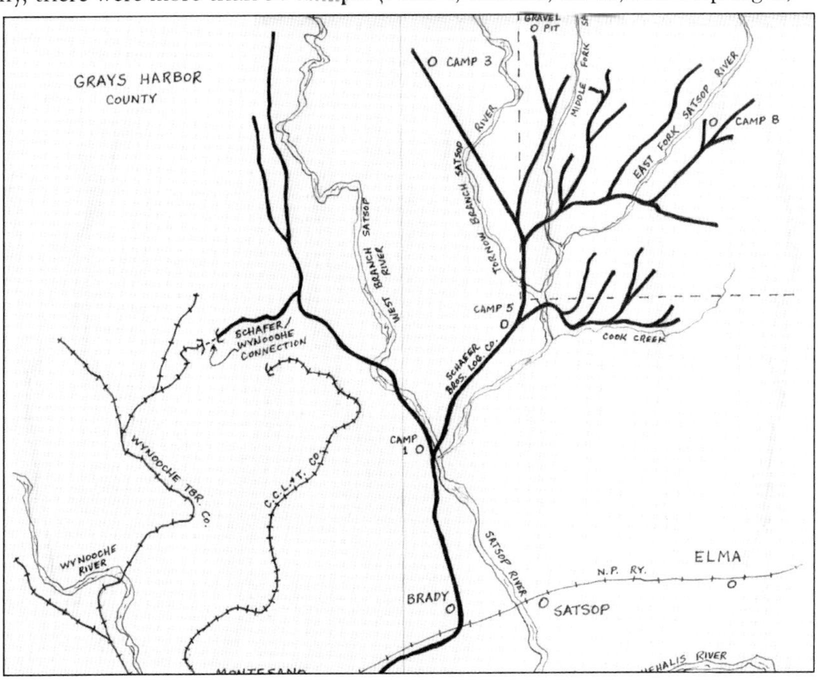

Schafer Camp One, a few miles north of Brady, served the Schafer railroad and provided a repair shop, a locomotive shop, and equipment manufacturing. It also housed much of the railroad equipment. The Schafer crew is seen here in 1920 sitting on a speeder car, which was used to get men and equipment to logging sites quickly and efficiently. (UW Libraries, C. Kinsey No. 3809.)

Although not round, Camp One was called a roundhouse and served as the engine house and repair facility. It was situated at the fork of the western and eastern branches of the Satsop River, where the roads were named for the branches. By 1920, some of the employees were able to drive to work in their cars. This sign in the foreground points to Montesano, Matlock, and Camp One. (Chehalis Museum.)

Here, in 1920, a Schafer Bros. Company loading crew poses on one of the huge logs, which would be loaded on a railroad car and taken to the Chehalis River, where it could be carried downstream to the mills in Montesano or Aberdeen. A spar tree stands upright behind the men and the donkey engine, which powered the cables to move the logs. (UW Libraries, C. Kinsey No. 3625.)

At Camp Three, temporary construction was used so the bunkhouses and other camp buildings could easily be transferred to a flatbed railcar or a truck and quickly moved to the next logging site. (UW Libraries, C. Kinsey No. 3624.)

Here, the camp office building is already loaded onto the railcar and ready to move to the next site. This is a rather refined building for a logging camp, with a fireplace chimney, well-made doors, and curtains on the windows. (UW Libraries, C. Kinsey No. 3652.)

A logging crew poses in front of the buildings at Camp Three in 1921. The camps were raised off the ground so they could be easily loaded onto railcars and so they would avoid the frequent flooding of the Satsop River. Camp crews like this one included women, who would likely have worked in the kitchen and dining hall. (Chehalis Museum.)

Camp Five, near Schafer State Park, became especially well known because, during World War I, it housed the first unit of the famous "Spruce Battalion," which was utilized to increase the production of lumber for the war effort. This 1924 photograph shows two babies at the far right, perhaps softening life at the rough-and-tumble camp. (Fuquay.)

In the 1920s, the sons of Peter and Marie Schafer had taken on prominent roles in the family logging operations. The Camp Six crew taking down this giant fir tree included, from left to right, "Eskimo Joe," Carl Schafer, Mint Look, John Schafer, and Ole Olson. (Fuquay.)

John and Carl Schafer look businesslike as they pose beside this giant fir tree, which was 11 feet in diameter, in 1924. (Fuquay.)

At Camp Six in the 1920s, the loading crew and donkey engines set a world record for loading logs on railroad cars. The inscription on this photograph states, "World's record for one side, 67 cars in 8 hours." Bert Turner was the crew foreman. (UW Libraries, C. Kinsey No. 3710.)

In 1922, Carl Schafer, the son of Peter and Marie Schafer, was the foreman of Camp Six. The camp consisted of bunkhouses, a dining hall, a tool and sharpening building, equipment buildings, and other miscellaneous buildings. Camp Six was moved several times in the 1920s; it is ready for its next move in this photograph. (Fuquay.)

It was at times difficult for employees to leave a camp to buy things, so it was often necessary to have a store connected to the camp office. The quality of the furnishings and equipment in the store, as well as the supplies available for sale, are apparent in this photograph of Camp Six. (Aberdeen Museum.)

Camp Seven, on the west branch of the Satsop River, was an early site for developing loading capabilities. Here, the loading crew has a donkey engine and two spar trees and the high climber is beginning his climb to the top of the tree, which he will cut off so cables can be attached. (UW Libraries, C. Kinsey No. 3712.)

Camp Eight, only a few miles north of Schafer State Park, was one of the few Schafer camps along the Satsop River that was in Mason County and not Grays Harbor County. These photographs, taken at slightly different times in the late 1920s, illustrate much about the camp organization. The photograph above shows the Schafer Bros. Company Engine No. 1, a Heisler locomotive. The camp dining room is a converted passenger railroad car. It appears that the structure in front of the dining car with men sitting on it was the cookhouse. The photograph below shows a large camp crew, including the kitchen crew. The buildings are elevated, with wood for the stoves stacked under the building. (Above, Chehalis Museum; below, UW Libraries, C. Kinsey No. 3737.)

While the camp mess hall generally served excellent food to the loggers, the facilities tended to be utilitarian. The men would have their plates on the table, with condiments serving platters, and bowls on the upper level. Jim Devine, one of the Schafer Bros. Company chefs, was so famous in the area that he later operated a popular restaurant, The Coffee Cup, in Aberdeen. (Aberdeen Museum.)

The donkey engine and crew are at Camp 11, which was in the Wynoochee River Valley, the next valley west of the Satsop River Valley. The Wynoochee contained a long and winding river as well. Despite hills in between, the two valleys are only a few miles apart in places, so the Schafer Bros. Company could easily move camps between the valleys. (UW Libraries, C. Kinsey No. 3802.)

Camp 15, like many of the camps, was a railroad camp with camp buildings placed adjacent to the rail lines. Since the only traffic on the railroad was Schafer crews, the noise was not a problem because the crews were out in the woods working when the trains came by. Except for the women from the mess hall crew, in the middle back, the crew was entirely male. It is unlikely that families were living in the camp at this time. (UW Libraries, C. Kinsey No. 3621.)

This Schafer Bros. Company loading crew worked out of Camp 20, which was probably near Oakville in southeastern Grays Harbor County. Railroad tracks run behind the tree; the various cables shown would be connected to a donkey engine to pull the logs to be loaded onto the railroad car. (UW Libraries, C. Kinsey No. 3622.)

Once the logs were delivered to the log dump on the Satsop River, they would be joined into a log boom and towed down the Chehalis River to a mill in Montesano. Here, the Schafer Bros. Company tugboat, *Hoquiam*, moves the logs into place on the Chehalis River at the mill in Montesano. (Replinger.)

As early as 1923, there were children in some of the camps. However, it was still unusual to keep bear cubs as pets. Eight-year-old Muriel Murphy Moore, the daughter of Aberdeen attorney William J. Murphy, is seen in these photographs with bear cubs on leashes at what was probably Camp Six. Below, Muriel watches the cubs with her cousins Ralph and Kathryn Valentine. (Both, Sharon Moore.)

Written on this photograph, taken at one of the Schafer Bros. Company camps in the 1920s, is the following quote: "What do you think about it? She sure can go too! Jake's new car." A Chevrolet insignia can be seen on the radiator. "Jake" was probably a foreman or better if he could afford a flashy car like this one. (Fuquay.)

When the Schafer property was first donated to the City of Montesano, a celebration was held on August 22, 1922, to mark the dedication. Hundreds of friends, employees, well-wishers, and public officials attended. The Schafer Bros. Company band provided entertainment to the assemblage. (UW Libraries, C. Kinsey No. 3867.)

THIS INDENTURE Made this twenty-third day of February, nineteen hundred and twenty-four;

WITNESSETH:-- That SCHAFER BROS. LOGGING COMPANY, a corporation, organized and existing, under and by virtue of the laws of the State of Washington, and having its principal place of busines at Satsop, Grays Harbor County, State of Washington, the party of the first part, for and in consideration of the sum of ONE DOLLAR, lawful money of the United States of America, to it in hand paid by the STATE OF WASHINGTON, party of the second part, receipt of which is hereby acknowledged, does by these presents, grant, bargain, sell, alien, remise, release, convey and confirm unto the said party of the second part all of the following described real estate situated in Mason --------County, State of Washington to-wit:--

All that part of the South one-half ($S\frac{1}{2}$) of the bSouthwest quarter ($SW\frac{1}{4}$) of Section twenty-nine (29), Township nineteen (19), North range six (6) West of the Willamette Meridian, lying south of the Satsop River,

Together with all and singular, the tenements, hereditaments and appurtenances belonging or appertaining thereto,

TO HAVE AND TO HOLD the same to the said party of the second part as long as the same be used for a public park, and to revert to the party of the first part, its successors or assigns, should the party of the second part attempt to dispose of the same, or make use of it for any other purposes than a public park for the free enjoyment of the public.

IN WITNESS WHEREOF the said party of the first part, pursuant to and by authority of a resolution of its Board of Directors, and entered on its records, that it caused its corporate name to be subscribed hereto, on the day and year first above written.

SCHAFER BROS. LOGGING COMPANY
a, corporation,
By Peter Schafer Pres.

ATTEST: By Hubert Schafer Sect.

In 1922, Peter, Hubert, and Albert Schafer donated property on the Satsop River to the City of Montesano to establish a park. Over the next two years, it was decided that it would be better to donate the property to Washington State for a park to honor their parents, Anna and John D. Schafer. In February 1924, the deed was executed and the property became part of the Washington State Parks system. (Schafer.)

For the dedication in 1924, the three Schafer sons erected the monument above at the entrance to the park. The plaque in the monument reads, "Honoring the memory of John D. and Anna Schafer, Pioneers of 1870. This park is dedicated by their sons Peter, Hubert and Albert in 1924." The monument is still in good condition and remains at the entrance to the park today. (Schafer.)

MONTESANO STATE BANK

CAPITAL AND SURPLUS $100,000.00

MONTESANO, WASH. Aug.10th 1925.

C.V.Savidge,
Olympia, Wash.,

My Dear Clark:-

I beg to write you relative to the Schafer Park, which was donated to the ~~State~~ last year by Schafer Bros., .

I was just called up about the park this P.M., do not know why they called me, unlessit was I was mixed up with the proposition last year, when the donation was made, the party said that the park was not being kept up, the farmers had a big pi-picnic last week, they had about three thousand there, and I guess they left the park in rather an unkept condition, possibly is the reason it is in the condition it is, there is to be another big picnic there next week.

I am passing this along to you, for I know that you are one of the Park Board, and you can use your own good judgement in the matter, I know nothing about the condition of the park from personal obeservation, I know that there are a great many people there all during the summer.

With kindpersonal regards.

I beg to remain sincerelly yours,

W.H. France

In this letter, Mr. W.H. France, a prominent local banker, describes some of the difficulties for a heavily used park in the early days. Although Schafer State Park was a part of the state parks system, cleaning and maintaining it was still a problem. In the 1920s and 1930s, the park was popular with large groups, some of them numbering between 4,000 and 6,000 people, who did not always pick up after themselves. (State Archives.)

OFFICIAL PAPER
County of Grays Harbor

Vidette Aug 15, 1924 NUMBER 33.

MORE THAN TWO THOUSAND GO TO SCHAFER PICNIC

Editor of Timber Magazine Urges Boosting Reforestation

Between 2,500 and 3,000 people attended the picnic of Schafer Brothers Employes' Association Sunday at Schafer park at the fish hatchery. It was a most successful family gathering, attended by employes and friends who seemed to be enjoying themselves to the utmost. Details were handled well and the affair went off smoothly and orderly.

The contests and races were the chief attractions of the day and hundreds of dollars' worth of prizes were dispensed, all donated by friends of the Schafer concern. At noon, every one on the grounds was treated to a generous lunch and their plates heaped full of good things to eat. Two concerts by the Schafer band pleased the crowd immensely.

George M. Cornwall, editor of the Timberman of Portland, was the speaker of the day. Mr. Cornwall made a short and forceful address, stressing the need of reforestation and protection against fires.

"Unless you women and children here urge your public officers to give the proper attention to the forests, there will be no lumber men's picnics in years to come, for there will be no lumber industry here."

there will be no lumber industry here."

On Oriental Situation

Mr. Cornwall also spoke of the Oriental situation, saying that Japan would have to realize that she must make amends to China and work hand in hand with it; that she would have to adopt English as the official language as it was the working tool of commerce; and that we ought to consider at all times if we are treating the Orient fairly, for here was a great market for the United States.

There were many events that were not on the program and the prize winners were so numerous that it was impossible to keep track of them. However, the winners on the program events are as follows:

Men's 50 yard dash—Ed Schafer first; Carl Schafer, second; B. P. Hayden, third.

Fat men's race—Russell Hoyt, first John Pavich, second; H. M. Taylor, third; B. Shore, fourth.

Married ladies' race—Mrs. B. Ford, first; Mrs. A. Benson, second; Mrs. C. W. Eddy, third.

Single ladies' race—Bessie Eddy, first Opal Brock, second; Florence Mason, third.

Boys under 10 race—John Jepson, first Kenneth Turner, second.

Girls under 10—Mary Kelsey, first; Elsie Thompson, second; Gladys Eddy, third.

Speed race—Ed Schafer, first; Kenneth Williams, second.

Boys under 14 50 yard dash—Bernard Smith, first; Ed Muller, second Glen Meadows, third.

Girls 14 and under—Opal Brock, first; Una Lambert, second; Glata Lamber, third.

Boys 8 and under—John Jepson, first; Clarence Ballard, second.

Sack Races

Boys 8 and under—John Jepson, first; Clarence Ballard, second.

Sack Races

Boys 10 and under sack race—Taylor Hayden, first John Jeppson, second.

Boys 14 and under sack race—Ed Miller, first; William Johnson, second.

Girls 8 and under 25 yard dash—Geneva Ehrhart, first; Louise Johnson, second.

Men's 50 yard rush—Ken. Williams, first; John Leboke, second; Carl Schafer, third.

Skirt race—Bessie Eddy, first; Opal Brock, second Florence Mason, third.

Pie eating contest—Ralph Look, first; William Johnson, second.

Cracker eating contest—Joe Moore, first; Glen Meadows, second.

Largest family on grounds—J. A. Townsend, first; H. B. Thompson, second.

Man with shiniest dome—Robert Morgan, first; S. S. Tripp, second.

Oldest man employe in service—Al Barrett, first Rusy Phillips, second; Ed Kesterson, third.

Oldest lady employe—Margaret Maloney, first; Adrian King, second.

Broad jump—Mint Look, first; Bert Turner, second; Bob Ford, third.

High jump — Ralph Williams, first; I. W. Urquhart, second; Bob Larm, third.

Girls' race — Florence Mason, first; opal Brock, second; Glata Lambert, third.

Dancing—Mr. and Mrs. M. Ulshaffer, first; Mr. and Mrs. Bob Ford, second; Mr .and Mrs. H. Phillips, third.

The *Montesano Vidette* was the newspaper of record for Grays Harbor County in the 1920s. It never failed to give extensive coverage to the Schafer Bros. Company employee picnic at Schafer State Park, before and after the event. This article from August 15, 1924, provides some idea of the wide range of events and games that took place at the picnics. (The *Montesano Vidette*.)

Here, the photographer has caught the eye of some of the spectators watching the games and contests at the employee picnic. (Aberdeen Museum.)

The Schafer Bros. Company held annual picnics at Schafer State Park from the early 1900s until the company was sold in 1955. In preparation for the picnic, the employees would build a dam across the river, build docks and stands for spectators, organize food and drink, and arrange for games and entertainment. Here, spectators watch a log-rolling contest from a temporary dock. (UW Libraries, C. Kinsey No. 3773.)

Since the early 1900s, a bridge has spanned the Satsop River to provide a crossing for residents and later for visitors to the park. In 1907, a fish hatchery was constructed next to what became Schafer State Park. The hatchery weir is seen here, lined with some of the several thousand people who came for the annual picnic in 1926. (Schafer.)

One of the most popular and exciting events at the annual employee picnic was the greased-pole walking contest. For this contest, a long, skinny log was secured to the riverbank and pointed out over the river. The pole was heavily greased and contestants were told to walk out to the end. Few, if any, made it all the way to the end, so falls into the river were common. (State Archives.)

The race is on and the swimmers are headed for the finish line in this photograph. The man with the megaphone would ensure that no one cheated and inform the spectators about the winner and all the participants. (Aberdeen Museum.)

Peter Schafer spent much of his early life on and around the Satsop River. He was a great boatman, fisherman, and swimmer. He is seen here in a suit, tie, and hat at the annual picnic in the park in 1926, demonstrating his poling skills for a young passenger. This canoe was built in the Indian style and was hollowed out of a single cedar log. (State Archives.)

The Schafer Bros. Company band, made up of employees and friends, provided entertainment in the Grays Harbor County area for many years. They held concerts, participated in parades, and were available for other local events. Of course, they were also regular participants at the annual picnics held at Schafer State Park. (Both, Aberdeen Museum.)

Here, the crowd at the Schafer Bros. Company employee picnic has begun to move toward the kitchens for lunch. It took enormous planning and preparation to be able to feed the 4,000 to 6,000 employees, families, and friends who commonly joined the picnic. (Aberdeen Museum.)

Food and drink were important components of the annual employee picnic. In addition to setting up kitchens and providing good food and drink—loggers expected the food to be as good as what they were served in the camps—the employees erected shelters and provided hundreds of picnic tables. (Aberdeen Museum.)

Games, races, and contests of skill provided much of the entertainment at the annual picnics. There were races for men, boys, ladies, girls under 10, and even "fat men." A wooden platform was built along the river for the footraces. The ladies ran in their long skirts and dresses, and some even kept their hats on. (State Archives.)

Members of the Schafer family enjoyed visiting Schafer State Park even in the colder months of the year. Seen here in the late 1920s sitting in front of the monument at the entrance to the park are, from left to right, Marie Schafer; Edwin Hobi, who would later marry Marie's sister Gertrude; Trudy Gleason; and Trudy's mother, Anna Gleason. (Schafer.)

Seen here at Schafer State Park in the late 1920s are, from left to right, Anna Schafer Gleason, Trudy Gleason, Marie Schafer, and Harold Reid. Marie Schafer and Harold Reid would later marry. The park's bridge over the Satsop River is in the background. (Schafer.)

Early in the 1900s, the Schafers built a dance hall on the property that was later donated for Schafer State Park. Local newspaper accounts reported on the many dances held there for local residents. In 1922, volunteers from the Montesano Chamber of Commerce built a roof on the hall and it became even more in demand for dances and events. This photograph was taken by famous Pacific Northwest photographer Asahel Curtis. (Washington State Parks.)

Logging in the forests along the Satsop River and in the Olympic Mountains required more than going into the woods with saws and axes. The Schafer Bros. Company not only needed loggers but also carpenters, builders, engineers, and planners. Railroad lines often needed trestles to move from one high area to the next, and each trestle had to be built by the Schafer Bros. Company, as opposed to the state government. (Chehalis Museum.)

The enormous loads that were carried and pulled by the locomotives are seen in this 1926 photograph. The caption reads, "104 cars containing 875,000 feet of timber. Worlds record for one side in 8 hours." Note the man standing at the left of the photograph waving to the train. (UW Libraries, C. Kinsey No. 3843.)

The height and size of some of the trestles built by the Schafer Bros. Company were enormous. This bridge and trestle crossing the Satsop River was likely more than 100 feet high. (Fuquay.)

Once the train with the load of logs reached the river, it would enter an angled log dump where the logs could be easily off-loaded from the railroad car into the river. Once in the river, the logs would be gathered into booms and towed down the river to the mill. (Aberdeen Museum.)

This Heisler locomotive is designated "No. 1" on the front of the engine. It is likely the first engine the Schafer Bros. Company owned. This photograph shows the same load of 104 railroad cars with a record footage of logs shown on the trestle in the previous photograph. (Chehalis Museum.)

This photograph offers a good idea of how the giant donkey engines might be moved around in the woods in the early days. The donkey engine was mounted on skids, and a cable would be hooked to a tree beyond the intended site, and then the donkey engine would pull the donkey along with the cable. (UW Libraries, C. Kinsey No. 3750.)

A high climber begins his ascent up a 250-foot fir tree. On his heavy belt, he carries an ax and a saw. He will flip the rope up each time he moves to the next level on the tree. The climbing irons fastened to his legs allow him to maintain traction as he ascends, chopping or sawing off tree limbs as he goes to the top. (Jones No. 17,367.)

In order to make the spar on which to hook cables to move the logs, a high climber, wearing climbing irons and with a large belt holding axes and saws and other tools, climbs to the top of the tree, cutting limbs along the way. Near the top of the tree, he saws off the top 20 or 30 feet of the tree to make a flat surface for the cable connections. It was a tradition among climbers to then climb on the topped tree and, without any safety gear, do a little dance. The climber can be seen here 250 feet above the ground with his arms outstretched, standing on top of the fir tree. (State Archives.)

Two steam donkeys have loaded their train with enormous logs in 1923. The spar with cables and chokers has been used to pull the logs out of the nearby woods and then place them on the railroad cars. On Labor Day 1923, this crew set another loading record. (Jones No. 5090.)

The Schafer Bros. Company logging crew poses at the base of a 425-year-old Douglas fir tree. The tree is more than 300 feet high, with a diameter of 10 feet. Albert Schafer is standing at the far right. Peter Schafer is standing second from the right. John Schafer is fourth from the right leaning against the tree between two saws. (Fuquay.)

Giant log piles were often made by design, as the loading crew needed to bring the logs to a loading area to wait until the train was ready to take them to the mill. Such piles were also made when the river flooded and carried logs from the woods downriver until they were blocked. The men in this photograph look like dolls placed on the giant logs. (Chehalis Museum.)

Workers from China, Japan, and other parts of Asia played an important role in the development of the Schafer Bros. Company logging operations. Asian workers were especially important in building the railroad lines that stretched into the woods, making it possible for the long trains to bring out the logs. The Asian workers generally lived in separate camps from other workers. The camps, however, were comfortable and served their residents well. Although there were few Asian women in the woods in the 1920s, this camp obviously had at least one woman, who likely worked in the kitchen. (Both, UW Libraries, C. Kinsey No. 3639, No. 3684.)

In addition to their efforts to obtain wholesale customers by entertaining them at their game farm and on the yacht *Dreamerie*, the Schafer Bros. Company also began an active advertising campaign to attract local residents in the Grays Harbor County area to buy their lumber. This advertisement ran in the *Montesano Vidette* in 1927. (The *Montesano Vidette*.)

The Schafer Bros. Company foremen were not always dressed in lumberjack gear. The foremen are seen here in their best suits in front of the Schafer Bros. Company administration offices in Montesano. They are, from left to right, (first row) John Schafer, Russell Hoyt, Walt Robertson, Herman Maas, Elmer Due, Bert Turner, Al Barrett, Jim Maloney, Bob Ford, Mike Thomas, and Dave Brown; (second row) Mike Dovilich, Sam Musgrove, Claude Jamison, Ralph Loomis, and Jim Thayer. (UW Libraries, C. Kinsey No. 3731.)

Hubert Schafer died in 1931. His older brother and his younger brother lived on until 1945. In the late 1920s, the three brothers, who founded the Schafer Bros. Company together, sat for a formal studio portrait. From left to right, they are Peter, Albert, and Hubert Schafer. (Jones No. 6218.)

Four

The Depression Years of the 1930s

Members of the Schafer family enjoy a sunny summer day picnic at Schafer State Park. The small shelter built by the Works Progress Administration (WPA) is in the background. The photograph includes Maurice Schafer, the son of Albert, standing on the right; John Schafer, at the far end of the table on the left; Edward Schafer, at the far end of the table on the right; Peter and Marie Schafer, fifth and sixth from the far end on the right; and Timothy Gleason, in front on the left with several children from the next generation on his left. (Jones No. 15,771.)

Throughout the 1920s, 1930s, and 1940s, the Schafer Bros. Company expanded its lumber operations by buying or building mills in Montesano, Aberdeen, and Hoquiam. The interior of the Montesano shingle mill is seen here in an unusually clear and light photograph; mills were often very dark inside. (Chehalis Museum.)

The Schafer Bros. Company Mill No. 3 was a primary producer of high-quality cedar shingles. Shingles to be shipped by rail were loaded onto kiln cars and placed in the kilns for drying. If the shingles were to be shipped by sea, they would be shipped green and wait for drying at their destination. (Chehalis Museum.)

The Schafer Bros. Company Mill No. 4, in Aberdeen, produced a large volume of finished lumber that was shipped all over the United States by rail and sent to Asia or along the West Coast by ship. The high volume of shipping is seen here, with several barges and motor vessels pulled up at the mill dock. The Weyerhauser Company acquired the mill in 1955 and continued to use it into the early 2000s. (Chehalis Museum.)

The Schafer Bros. Company cargo ship *Margaret Schafer* was named for John Schafer's daughter. In 1936, it carried the largest shipment of certigrade red cedar shingles from Grays Harbor. In the 1950s, the ship became a movie star when it was used in the film *The Sea Chase* starring John Wayne and Lana Turner. (Jones No. 15,840.)

The *Margaret Schafer* is seen here steaming out of Aberdeen, heavily laden with a load of lumber bound for Hawaii or a West Coast port. (Jones No. 21,338.)

The Schafer Bros. Company's steel tug *Maurine* was named after Albert Schafer's daughter. It worked on the Chehalis River for many years until it was taken over by the US government during World War II. In 1943, it was lost at sea with all hands on board. (Chehalis Museum.)

This Douglas fir tree was about 425 years old, 300 feet tall, 127 feet to the first limb, 10 feet and 10 inches in diameter, and provided 49,669 board feet of lumber. Seated in front of the tree in this 1936 photograph are, from left to right, Ben Kesterson, John Schafer, Peter Schafer, and Albert Schafer. Tools are shown leaning against the tree and fallers have already started a cut. (Chehalis Museum.)

This photograph shows the same tree after a large cut was made in it. The tree was felled by Pat Miller and Gus Quick and was bucked and cut into standard lengths by Frank Hafferty. (Jones No. 14,456.)

In the late 1800s and early 1900s, the loggers in Grays Harbor County were amazed by the size of the fir trees in the forests there. The diameters of some trees were so large that after the tree was cut down, the remaining stump was turned into a house. This early stump house was moved in the 1930s to John Schafer's home on Hood Canal and was used as a bathhouse. (Schafer.)

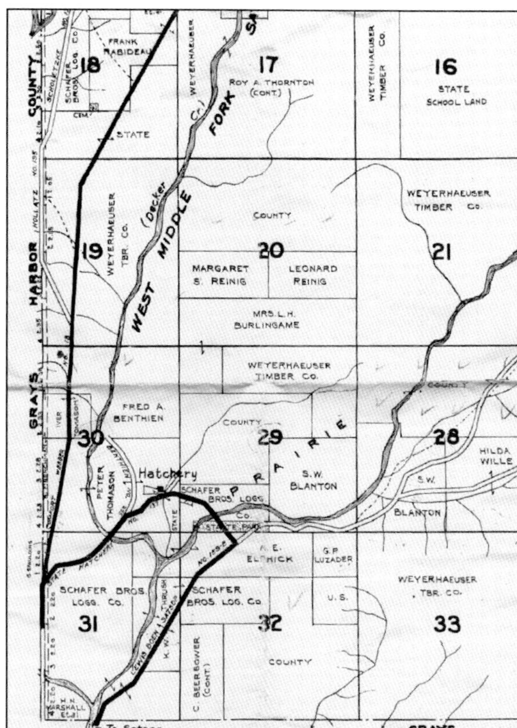

By the 1930s, the Schafer Bros. Company still owned forest property in the area surrounding Schafer State Park, but much of their holdings were farther afield in the Olympic Forest, along the Wynoochee River and in Lewis County. This 1935 Metzger map shows how ownership had changed in the Satsop River Valley around the park. (Michael Sinclair.)

Schafer family members continued to enjoy picnics at the park in the 1930s. Schafer family members are seen here with the dance hall in the background and children on the ladder. Seated on the ground is Carl Schafer's wife, Mabel; seated are Marie and Peter Schafer; and standing, from left to right, are Carl Schafer, Edward Schafer, Harold Reid, Marie Schafer Reid, Anna Schafer Gleason, Timothy Gleason, and Edward Schafer's wife, Ruth. (Schafer.)

In 1932, Marie Schafer, the daughter of Peter and Marie, married Harold "Had" Reid in Aberdeen. They had first met when Reid's building company, Reid Brothers Construction Company, was hired to build Peter Schafer's house in Aberdeen in the 1920s. (Schafer.)

Parades were great events in small-town America in the 1920s and 1930s. Aberdeen was no different, and the Schafer Bros. Company did not miss an opportunity to appear in and support the parade. Above, the company float carries an impressive depiction of the many facets of logging and lumbering. (Aberdeen Museum.)

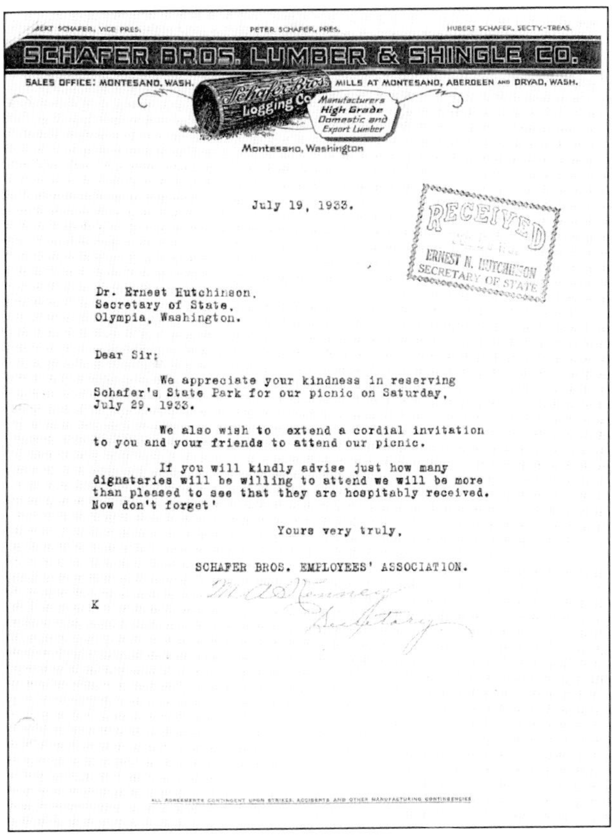

...BERT SCHAFER, VICE PRES. PETER SCHAFER, PRES. HUBERT SCHAFER, SECTY.-TREAS.

SCHAFER BROS. LUMBER & SHINGLE CO.

SALES OFFICE: MONTESANO, WASH. MILLS AT MONTESANO, ABERDEEN AND DRYAD, WASH.

Schafer Bros. Logging Co.

Manufacturers High Grade Domestic and Export Lumber

Montesano, Washington

July 19, 1933.

RECEIVED
ERNEST N. HUTCHINSON
SECRETARY OF STATE

Dr. Ernest Hutchinson,
Secretary of State,
Olympia, Washington.

Dear Sir:

We appreciate your kindness in reserving Schafer's State Park for our picnic on Saturday, July 29, 1933.

We also wish to extend a cordial invitation to you and your friends to attend our picnic.

If you will kindly advise just how many dignataries will be willing to attend we will be more than pleased to see that they are hospitably received. Now don't forget'

Yours very truly,

SCHAFER BROS. EMPLOYEES' ASSOCIATION.

K

ALL AGREEMENTS CONTINGENT UPON STRIKES, ACCIDENTS AND OTHER MANUFACTURING CONTINGENCIES

The Schafer Bros. Company Employees' Association was always very businesslike in organizing the annual picnic at Schafer State Park. It maintained good relations with the secretary of state, who oversaw parks operations, and it was expected that politicians and other dignitaries would not miss the opportunity to appear with several thousand workers and their families. (State Archives.)

In the 1930s, the Depression meant hardships and the loss of jobs for many residents of the Satsop River Valley. The annual picnics went on, however, and offered those still working the opportunity to enjoy themselves and be thankful that the Schafer Bros. Company was still operating. (Jones No. 15,775.)

At the Schafer Bros. Company annual employee picnic in 1938, one of the most popular contests was the ladies nail-pounding event. Many of the ladies spent long hours prior to the picnic honing their skills and getting tips from local carpenters. (Jones No. 15,763)

The Schafer Bros. Company loggers were well known in the community for their skills in all activities related to the water. Here, Elton Schmidt drives a large wooden ball made from a cedar tree at Schafer State Park in the 1930s. A similar cedar ball can be seen today at nearby Lake Sylvia State Park. (Jones No. 15,773.)

Competitive log rolling was a regular feature at Schafer picnics in the 1930s and earlier. Two competing loggers would wear their hobnail boots for traction, spin the log back and forth, make quick stops, and do everything they could to knock their opponent off the log. (Jones No. 15,772.)

The creative minds of the loggers did not rest between the annual employee picnics. They were continually thinking up and developing contests to entertain the picnickers and show off their prowess. In 1938, pole boxing in small boat-like contraptions was the newest event. (Jones No. 15,762.)

During the Great Depression, the Civil Works Administration and the Works Progress Administration (WPA) constructed a number of buildings at Schafer State Park, many of which still stand today. Fred Russell was the manager of Schafer State Park at the time and supervised much of the work. (State Archives.)

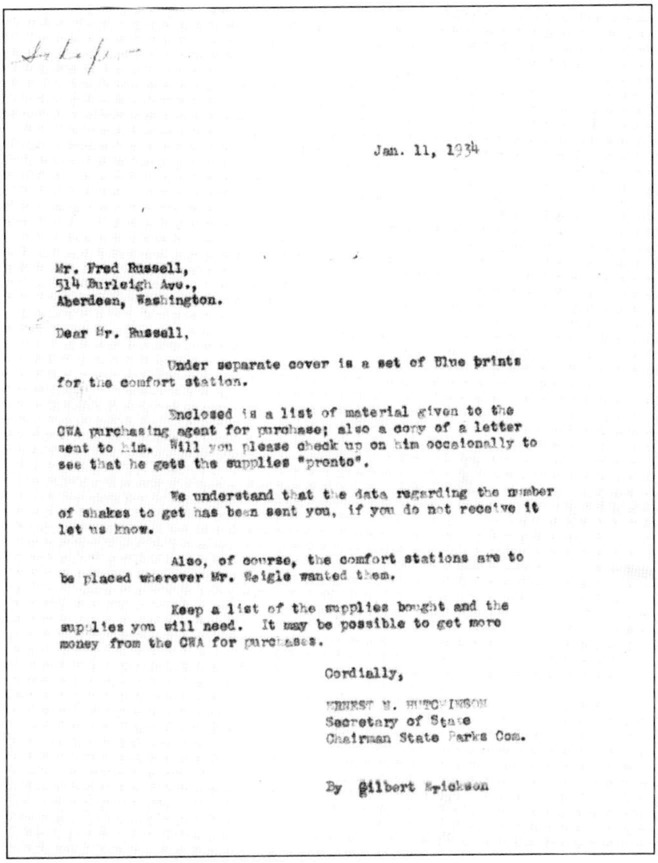

Jan. 11, 1934

Mr. Fred Russell,
514 Burleigh Ave.,
Aberdeen, Washington.

Dear Mr. Russell,

Under separate cover is a set of Blue prints for the comfort station.

Enclosed is a list of material given to the CWA purchasing agent for purchase; also a copy of a letter sent to him. Will you please check up on him occasionally to see that he gets the supplies "pronto".

We understand that the data regarding the number of shakes to get has been sent you, if you do not receive it let us know.

Also, of course, the comfort stations are to be placed wherever Mr. Weigle wanted them.

Keep a list of the supplies bought and the supplies you will need. It may be possible to get more money from the CWA for purchases.

Cordially,

ERNEST N. HUTCHINSON
Secretary of State
Chairman State Parks Com.

By Gilbert Erickson

In the 1930s, several "comfort stations," or restrooms (below), were built by WPA workers using local materials such as river rock, cedar shakes, and fir slabs. The stations still stand today and provide considerable "comfort" to park visitors. (Schafer.)

The Ranger's House at Schafer State Park was one of the important buildings erected by WPA workers in the 1930s. A notable construction aspect is the use of river rock for the walls, which was frowned upon by the National Park Service as being unstable. The Ranger's House remains standing today and is occupied by the current ranger and family. (Schafer.)

Another of the buildings erected by WPA workers is a small shelter with a wood-burning stove. The same craftsmanship and attention to detail found in the other buildings is evident in the simple but elegant structure, which still stands today. The stove has recently been renovated by local volunteers. (Schafer.)

Baseball was an important recreational activity in the 1920s and 1930s. Many local businesses sponsored teams and the competition was keen. The Schafer Bros. Company was no exception, and the company team usually wound up near the top of the standings at the end of the season. Some of the participants in this photograph are Albert Schafer (kneeling, far left) and, standing, Bob Mock (far left), Maurice Schafer (second from left), and Carl Schafer (second from right). (Schafer.)

In the early 1930s, the Schafer Bros. Company promised its baseball players that if they came in first in their league, they would be treated to a cruise to Canada on the company yacht, the *Dreamerie.* When the team won the title, the company kept its promise, and the team is seen here on board for its two-week trip to Canada. (Garold Messenger.)

Five

World War II to the Present

In 1940, as part of the dedication of the new Olympic logging camp, the family leadership of the company posed in front of one of their locomotive engines. Standing from left to right are Maurice Schafer, son of Albert; Edward Schafer, son of Peter; Gerald Schafer, son of Hubert; Albert and Peter Schafer, the two surviving brothers who started the company; Frank Schafer, son of Hubert; and Carl and John Schafer, sons of Peter. (Jones No. 17,366.)

This aerial photograph shows the Schafer Bros. Company buildings, railroad center, and shops in Brady. The photograph was taken shortly before the company was sold to Simpson Timber Company, of Shelton, Washington, in 1955. (Chehalis Museum.)

Schafer Olympic Camp: Up the Satsop

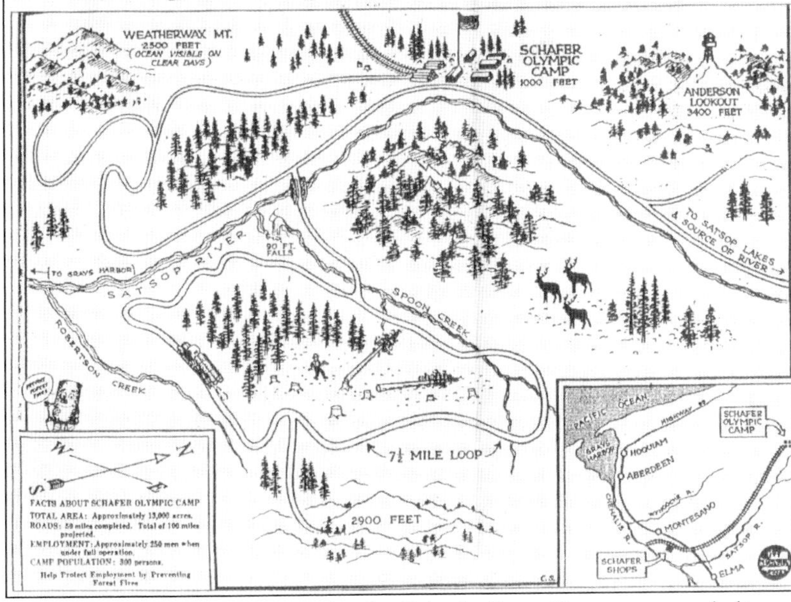

Shown in the Sept. 6, 1951 *Vidette*: Writer Dorothy Latimer describing her Schafer Camp adventures.

A new, modern logging camp for the Schafer Bros. Company was dedicated in 1940. The map and drawing appeared in the *Montesano Vidette* at the time and was republished in the *Vidette* in 1951. Such a camp required housing, a cookhouse, a shop building, lights, storage sheds, water and sewage systems, and railroad yards. Additionally, the buildings had to be constructed to withstand snowfall of eight feet or more. (The *Montesano Vidette*.)

In 1940, the Schafer Bros. Company offered a treat to the staffs at their main office in Aberdeen, at their Aberdeen Plywood Company, and at their Acme Door Company. They were to be taken by speeder car 30 miles on the railroad track to the Olympic Camp to see the logging operation firsthand and enjoy a real camp meal. Along with the staff in this photograph are John Schafer (far left), Carl Schafer (far right), and Edward Schafer (sitting in the middle front). (Chehalis Museum.)

Ben Kesterson, the pioneer Satsop River Valley logger who showed Peter, Hubert, and Albert Schafer how to log the big trees of the area, was honored in 1940 at the annual Schafer Bros. Company picnic at Schafer State Park. Kesterson became the prime timber cruiser for the company. The job of the cruiser was to estimate the quality and quantity of standing timber in an area to be logged. (Jones No. 17,376.)

As America began preparing for war, the Schafer Bros. Company steamship, the SS *Anna Schafer*, was taken over by the Navy. On January 3, 1942, the following message was sent to Carl Schafer from the ship's chief engineer, John J. McGee: "*Anna* now painted gray leaving tomorrow morning with *Margaret* to join convoy from Seattle about thirty miles out. Convoy to include about thirty odd ships." (Aberdeen Museum.)

In 1942, the Schafer Bros. Company used an electric transfer log loader. Mechanization of logging operations was well on its way by this time. It was a far cry from the oxen teams first used for logging in 1895. Here, from left to right, are Helen Schafer, Nita Schafer, Mabel Schafer, and Albert Schafer. (Fuquay.)

In the summer of 1942, the Schafer family and friends are shown at Hood Canal. Adults seen here, from left to right, are (first row) Carl Schafer, Mabel Schafer, Anna Schafer Gleason, Ruth Schafer, Marie Schafer, Peter Schafer, Gertrude Schafer Hobi, and John Schafer; (second row) Harold Reid, Edwin Hobi, Frank Schafer, Marie Schafer Reid, Lena Muller, Herman Muller, Nita Schafer, and Velma Muller. (Schafer.)

The Harbor Plywood mill, established in 1925, was located at the port dock in Aberdeen. During World War II, it was the largest plywood mill in the world. Because of the Depression, the number of mills in Aberdeen had declined from 37 to nine, but Harbor Plywood continued to produce an enormous amount of plywood. The Schafer Bros. Company supplied Harbor Plywood with peeler logs to turn into plywood. (Jones No. 14,484-2.)

World War II saw many changes in the workforce, including the employment of women in the lumber mills in Aberdeen and Hoquiam. The women in these photographs are working on the conveyor belt at Harbor Plywood, where the Schafer Bros. Company supplied the logs for fabrication into plywood. As the huge slabs of plywood came down the chain, the women pulled and stacked them, often without gloves or other safety equipment. Once the war ended and soldiers returned to work in the mills, they replaced the women who had worked during the war. (Left, State Archives; below, Jones No. 17,605.)

1944

SCHAFER BROS.

Annual

Employee's Banquet

Wednesday, November 8th

Morck Hotel

Aberdeen, Washington

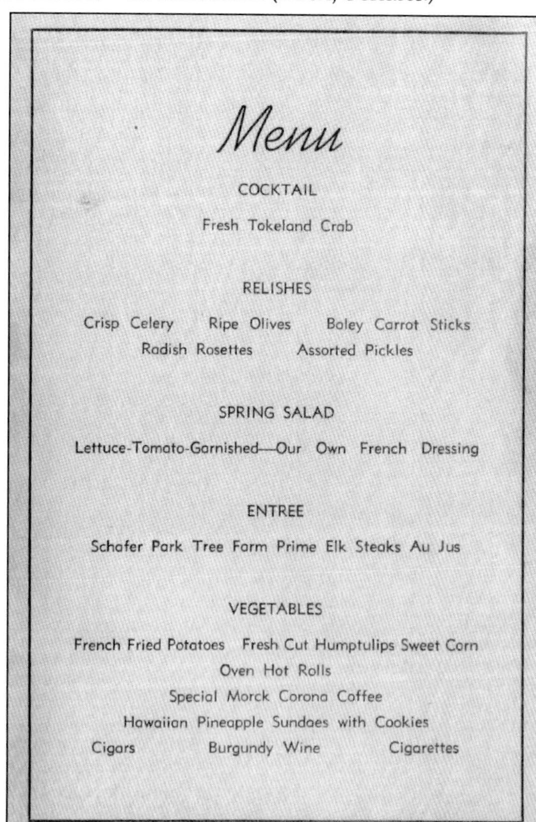

Menu

COCKTAIL

Fresh Tokeland Crab

RELISHES

Crisp Celery Ripe Olives Baley Carrot Sticks
Radish Rosettes Assorted Pickles

SPRING SALAD

Lettuce-Tomato-Garnished—Our Own French Dressing

ENTREE

Schafer Park Tree Farm Prime Elk Steaks Au Jus

VEGETABLES

French Fried Potatoes Fresh Cut Humptulips Sweet Corn
Oven Hot Rolls
Special Morck Corona Coffee
Hawaiian Pineapple Sundaes with Cookies
Cigars Burgundy Wine Cigarettes

The Morck Hotel in Aberdeen was a favorite place for banquets, dances, wedding receptions, teas, and other celebrations. Despite the ongoing war, the Schafer Bros. Company managed to continue holding the annual employees banquet in 1944. The menu featured many local food items such as Tokeland Crab, Baley carrot sticks, Schafer Park Tree Farm elk steaks, and Humptulips sweet corn. Although it was not local, the Hawaiian Pineapple may have come from one of the Schafer Bros. Company's customers in Honolulu. (Both, Schafer.)

In 1945, as the war was ending, a number of men in uniform are seen here at the annual employees banquet at the Morck Hotel in Aberdeen. Members of the Schafer family and corporate officers stand behind the head table at the back of the room. (Schafer.)

Standing at the head table in 1945 at the annual employees banquet are, among others, from left to right, Jack Close, the husband of Maurine Schafer, in his Navy uniform; Nita Schafer; Mabel Schafer; Maurice Schafer, in his uniform; Vance Schafer; Gerald Schafer, an unidentified couple in the corner; Helen and Albert Schafer; an unidentified man; Maureen Schafer Close; Edward Schafer; Marie Schafer Reid; John Schafer; Ruth Schafer; Carl Schafer; and Harold Reid. (Schafer.)

In 1942, John, Carl, Edward, and Maurice Schafer started the Grays Harbor Prefab Company, which made doors and pallet boards. In 1945, the company bought Alderbrook, a well-known resort on Hood Canal. This aerial photograph was taken by Stan Spiegel in 1948. The Schafers made many improvements, including razing the tent cabins and replacing them with permanent cottages. (Jones No. L31RH11F6_1.)

The main lodge at Alderbrook Inn was a rustic, wooden, mostly one-story structure with a few rooms for staff at one end of the second floor. In the 1920s and 1930s, Alderbrook was a popular destination and could be reached by both water and land. The parking lot was often filled with guests' cars, and many boats were tied up at the dock. (The Alderbrook Inn Collection.)

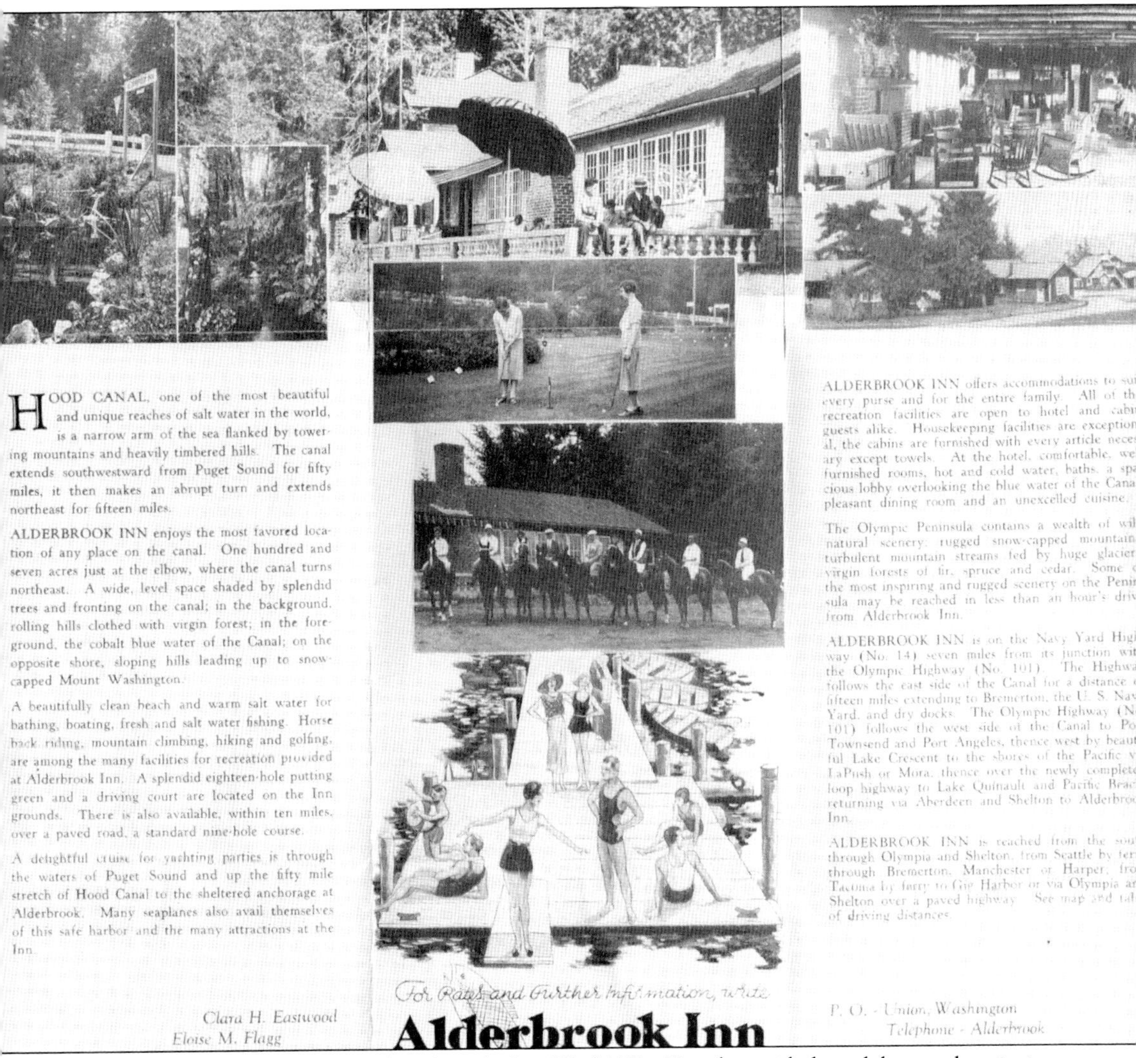

HOOD CANAL, one of the most beautiful and unique reaches of salt water in the world, is a narrow arm of the sea flanked by towering mountains and heavily timbered hills. The canal extends southwestward from Puget Sound for fifty miles, it then makes an abrupt turn and extends northeast for fifteen miles.

ALDERBROOK INN enjoys the most favored location of any place on the canal. One hundred and seven acres just at the elbow, where the canal turns northeast. A wide, level space shaded by splendid trees and fronting on the canal; in the background, rolling hills clothed with virgin forest; in the foreground, the cobalt blue water of the Canal; on the opposite shore, sloping hills leading up to snow-capped Mount Washington.

A beautifully clean beach and warm salt water for bathing, boating, fresh and salt water fishing. Horse back riding, mountain climbing, hiking and golfing, are among the many facilities for recreation provided at Alderbrook Inn. A splendid eighteen-hole putting green and a driving court are located on the Inn grounds. There is also available, within ten miles, over a paved road, a standard nine-hole course.

A delightful cruise for yachting parties is through the waters of Puget Sound and up the fifty mile stretch of Hood Canal to the sheltered anchorage at Alderbrook. Many seaplanes also avail themselves of this safe harbor and the many attractions at the Inn.

Clara H. Eastwood
Eloise M. Flagg

For Rates and Further Information, write

Alderbrook Inn

ALDERBROOK INN offers accommodations to sui every purse and for the entire family. All of th recreation facilities are open to hotel and cabi guests alike. Housekeeping facilities are exception al, the cabins are furnished with every article neces ary except towels. At the hotel, comfortable, wel furnished rooms, hot and cold water, baths, a spa cious lobby overlooking the blue water of the Cana pleasant dining room and an unexcelled cuisine.

The Olympic Peninsula contains a wealth of wil natural scenery: rugged snow-capped mountain turbulent mountain streams fed by huge glaciers virgin forests of fir, spruce and cedar. Some c the most inspiring and rugged scenery on the Penin sula may be reached in less than an hour's driv from Alderbrook Inn.

ALDERBROOK INN is on the Navy Yard High way (No. 14) seven miles from its junction wit the Olympic Highway (No. 101). The Highwa follows the east side of the Canal for a distance c fifteen miles extending to Bremerton, the U. S. Nav Yard, and dry docks. The Olympic Highway (N 101) follows the west side of the Canal to Po Townsend and Port Angeles, thence west by beaut ful Lake Crescent to the shores of the Pacific v LaPush or Mora, thence over the newly complete loop highway to Lake Quinault and Pacific Beac returning via Aberdeen and Shelton to Alderbroc Inn.

ALDERBROOK INN is reached from the sou through Olympia and Shelton, from Seattle by fer through Bremerton, Manchester or Harper, fro Tacoma by ferry to Gig Harbor or via Olympia an Shelton over a paved highway. See map and tal of driving distances.

P. O. - Union, Washington
Telephone - Alderbrook

This publicity brochure was produced just before World War II and provided an elaborate description of the many amenities at Alderbrook. In recent years, executives from the Microsoft Corporation have taken over the resort, razed the old lodge and bank of rooms, and added a swimming pool and a new, modern Craftsman-style lodge. (The Alderbrook Inn Collection.)

After World War II, it did not take long for parades to return as a staple of small-town life. The Schafer Bros. Company float, seen here at the corner of Wishkah and L Streets in Aberdeen, may not have won the grand prize, but there were some very cute children on board. (Aberdeen Museum.)

Schafer State Park ranger C.C. "Doc" Palmer is seen here with his wife, Rita, their children, Barbara and Stetson "Stet," and their dog, Lucky. They are standing in front of the Ranger's House at Schafer State Park in 1952. (Stetson Palmer.)

In the 1950s, C.C. "Doc" Palmer, was the ranger at Schafer State Park, where he lived with his family. New buildings were erected and many activities were renewed or initiated at the park in that decade. In January 1954, members of the Olympia Salmon Club had their annual salmon bake at the park. The filets of steelhead and salmon were cooked Native American–style over an open fire. The salmon bake eventually died out, but it has recently been revived by the Friends of Schafer and Lake Sylvia State Parks (FOSLS). (Stetson Palmer.)

The Satsop River at Schafer State Park remained a popular swimming spot, as seen in this 1950s photograph. Employee picnics continued, and the park was filled on most weekends in the summer. Today, the park remains a popular spot for families who want to enjoy its rural, natural setting. (Stetson Palmer.)

Although the fish hatchery at Schafer State Park was closed and moved upstream by the 1950s, the weir and salmon traps at the park remained usable for many years. Hatchery workers are seen here in the fish trap along the weir, capturing salmon to remove the eggs from the spawning fish. (Stetson Palmer.)

Hatchery workers are seen here in the mid-1950s at Schafer State Park with salmon they have taken from the trap. They will cut open the salmon, remove the eggs, and take them to the hatchery to be fertilized. The salmon are raised at the hatchery and, when they are old enough and strong enough, released into the river to begin their journey to the ocean. In a few years, they will return to the spot where they were released to repeat the cycle in one of nature's great stories. (Stetson Palmer.)

After the Schafer Bros. Company sold their business to the Simpson Timber Company, Carl Schafer, the son of Peter and Marie, took over the old Schafer Game Farm and turned it into his home. On the farm, he built an extensive museum made up of Schafer family and company artifacts. In addition to the museum building—which displayed photographs, tools, documents, and memorabilia in well-organized display cases, on panels, and on walls—the museum also included many large items such as the old Schafer railroad locomotive engine and an early steam donkey engine. The museum no longer exists, but many of the artifacts are now on display at the Chehalis Valley History Museum in Montesano. (Both, Peter Schafer Reid.)

Another popular event at Schafer State Park in the 1950s and 1960s that has been revived is the annual Yule Log Celebration each December. A suitable log is hidden in the woods and children are sent out to find it. The one who finds it makes the first cut in the log. The log is then chopped in pieces, with one part burned and another saved for the next year's event. (Stetson Palmer.)

Once the Yule Log is cut and placed in the fireplace for burning, the fun begins. A potluck supper fills the tables, musical instruments are played, carols are sung, and stories are told. The hall has festive decorations and, with an occasional dusting of snow, everyone has a grand time. (Stetson Palmer.)

NATIONAL REGISTER OF HISTORIC PLACES

Washington State Advisory Council on Historic Preservation
and
United States Department of the Interior

In recognition of its significance to our cultural heritage,
the

Schafer State Park
in

Elma, Washington
has been entered in the National Register of Historic Places.

Date Entered:
May 10, 2010

THE SEAL OF THE STATE OF WASHINGTON 1889

Chairman
Advisory Council on Historic Preservation

State Historic Preservation Officer

In 2010, because of the many historic events at and around Schafer State Park, state and federal officials acted on an application from the Friends of Schafer and Lake Sylvia State Parks (FOSLS) and placed Schafer State Park in the State and National Registers of Historic Places. (FOSLS.)

In July 2010, Gerry Alexander, the chief justice of the Washington State Supreme Court, presided over the unveiling of the Historic Site plaque at Schafer State Park. A picnic was held and more than 600 Schafer relatives, friends, and members of the local community attended. The Grays Harbor Banjo Band provided entertainment and several local museums provided displays of early life and work in the Satsop River Valley. (Barbara Seal Ogle.)

Many Schafer family members attended the 2010 ceremony unveiling the plaque signifying Schafer State Park's new designation as a National Historic Place. Although the Schafer Bros. Company and its 6,000 employees and friends could not attend, many of the same games played at the picnics in the 1920s and 1930s were played. (Barbara Seal Ogle.)

In 2011, longtime Satsop River Valley resident Cliff Perry (standing in back with a pipe)—the husband of Betty Perry, a descendant of early pioneers Daniel and Johanna Gleason—poses with his grandson Justin Perry (standing directly in front of Cliff Perry) and friends with one day's catch of silver and coho salmon. The Satsop River continues the centuries-old fishing tradition today and remains a fertile, productive source of fish. (Cliff Perry.)